3111

2

ILLINOIS ▮▮▮▮ COLLEGE

A12901 898145

WITHDRAWN

OPPOSING VIEWPOINTS® SERIES

Copyright Infringement

W9-BXL-013

I.C.C. LIBRARY

DEMCO

Other Books of Related Interest:

Current Controversies Series

Blogs

Issues on Trial Series

Right To Private Property

Issues That Concern You Series

Plagiarism

Opposing Viewpoints Series

Cyber Crime

"Congress shall make
no law. . .abridging the
freedom of speech, or
of the press."

First Amendment to the U.S. Constitution

The basic foundation of our democracy is the First Amendment guarantee of freedom of expression. The Opposing Viewpoints Series is dedicated to the concept of this basic freedom and the idea that it is more important to practice it than to enshrine it.

OPPOSING
VIEWPOINTS®
SERIES

Copyright Infringement

Roman Espejo, Book Editor

GREENHAVEN PRESS
A part of Gale, Cengage Learning

I.C.C. LIBRARY

GALE
CENGAGE Learning™

Detroit • New York • San Francisco • New Haven, Conn • Waterville, Maine • London

K
1485
.C674
2009

GALE
CENGAGE Learning

Christine Nasso, *Publisher*
Elizabeth Des Chenes, *Managing Editor*

© 2009 Greenhaven Press, a part of Gale, Cengage Learning

Gale and Greenhaven Press are registered trademarks used herein under license.

For more information, contact:
Greenhaven Press
27500 Drake Rd.
Farmington Hills, MI 48331-3535
Or you can visit our Internet site at gale.cengage.com

ALL RIGHTS RESERVED.
No part of this work covered by the copyright herein may be reproduced, transmitted, stored, or used in any form or by any means graphic, electronic, or mechanical, including but not limited to photocopying, recording, scanning, digitizing, taping, Web distribution, information networks, or information storage and retrieval systems, except as permitted under Section 107 or 108 of the 1976 United States Copyright Act, without the prior written permission of the publisher.

For product information and technology assistance, contact us at

Gale Customer Support, 1-800-877-4253
For permission to use material from this text or product, submit all requests online at www.cengage.com/permissions

Further permissions questions can be emailed to permissionrequest@cengage.com

Articles in Greenhaven Press anthologies are often edited for length to meet page requirements. In addition, original titles of these works are changed to clearly present the main thesis and to explicitly indicate the author's opinion. Every effort is made to ensure that Greenhaven Press accurately reflects the original intent of the authors. Every effort has been made to trace the owners of copyrighted material.

Cover image courtesy of Silverander Communications.

LIBRARY OF CONGRESS CATALOGING-IN-PUBLICATION DATA

Copyright infringement / Roman Espejo, book editor.
p. cm. -- (Opposing viewpoints)
Includes bibliographical references and index.
ISBN 978-0-7377-4358-6 (hardcover)
ISBN 978-0-7377-4357-9 (pbk.)
1. Copyright infringement. I. Espejo, Roman, 1977-
K1485.C674 2009
346.04'82--dc22

2009003341

Printed in the United States of America
1 2 3 4 5 6 7 13 12 11 10 09

Contents

Chapter 3: What Are the Effects of Copyright Infringement?

Why Consider Opposing Viewpoints?

> *"The only way in which a human being can make some approach to knowing the whole of a subject is by hearing what can be said about it by persons of every variety of opinion and studying all modes in which it can be looked at by every character of mind. No wise man ever acquired his wisdom in any mode but this."*
>
> *John Stuart Mill*

In our media-intensive culture it is not difficult to find differing opinions. Thousands of newspapers and magazines and dozens of radio and television talk shows resound with differing points of view. The difficulty lies in deciding which opinion to agree with and which "experts" seem the most credible. The more inundated we become with differing opinions and claims, the more essential it is to hone critical reading and thinking skills to evaluate these ideas. Opposing Viewpoints books address this problem directly by presenting stimulating debates that can be used to enhance and teach these skills. The varied opinions contained in each book examine many different aspects of a single issue. While examining these conveniently edited opposing views, readers can develop critical thinking skills such as the ability to compare and contrast authors' credibility, facts, argumentation styles, use of persuasive techniques, and other stylistic tools. In short, the Opposing Viewpoints Series is an ideal way to attain the higher-level thinking and reading skills so essential in a culture of diverse and contradictory opinions.

In addition to providing a tool for critical thinking, Opposing Viewpoints books challenge readers to question their own strongly held opinions and assumptions. Most people form their opinions on the basis of upbringing, peer pressure, and personal, cultural, or professional bias. By reading carefully balanced opposing views, readers must directly confront new ideas as well as the opinions of those with whom they disagree. This is not to simplistically argue that everyone who reads opposing views will—or should—change his or her opinion. Instead, the series enhances readers' understanding of their own views by encouraging confrontation with opposing ideas. Careful examination of others' views can lead to the readers' understanding of the logical inconsistencies in their own opinions, perspective on why they hold an opinion, and the consideration of the possibility that their opinion requires further evaluation.

Evaluating Other Opinions

To ensure that this type of examination occurs, Opposing Viewpoints books present all types of opinions. Prominent spokespeople on different sides of each issue as well as well-known professionals from many disciplines challenge the reader. An additional goal of the series is to provide a forum for other, less known, or even unpopular viewpoints. The opinion of an ordinary person who has had to make the decision to cut off life support from a terminally ill relative, for example, may be just as valuable and provide just as much insight as a medical ethicist's professional opinion. The editors have two additional purposes in including these less known views. One, the editors encourage readers to respect others' opinions—even when not enhanced by professional credibility. It is only by reading or listening to and objectively evaluating others' ideas that one can determine whether they are worthy of consideration. Two, the inclusion of such viewpoints encourages the important critical thinking skill of objectively evaluating an author's credentials and bias. This evaluation will illuminate an author's reasons for taking a particular stance on an issue and will aid in readers' evaluation of the author's ideas.

It is our hope that these books will give readers a deeper understanding of the issues debated and an appreciation of the complexity of even seemingly simple issues when good and honest people disagree. This awareness is particularly important in a democratic society such as ours in which people enter into public debate to determine the common good. Those with whom one disagrees should not be regarded as enemies but rather as people whose views deserve careful examination and may shed light on one's own.

Thomas Jefferson once said that "difference of opinion leads to inquiry, and inquiry to truth." Jefferson, a broadly educated man, argued that "if a nation expects to be ignorant and free . . . it expects what never was and never will be." As individuals and as a nation, it is imperative that we consider the opinions of others and examine them with skill and discernment. The Opposing Viewpoints Series is intended to help readers achieve this goal.

David L. Bender and Bruno Leone,
Founders

Introduction

"Copyleft . . . offers the promise of bring-
ing more content onto the Internet by
supplying a third alternative for publi-
cation."

George H. Pike,
"What Is Right About a Copyleft?"
Information Today, *April 2002.*

"As a fundamental concept, copyright re-
mains, because copyleft can't work with-
out copyright."

Paul Lambert,
"In Defense of Copyleft,"
Wired, *February 2001.*

In September 1983, software developer Richard M. Stallman introduced the GNU Project to the public, which commenced the following January; GNU is an acronym for "GNU's not Unix." Compatible with Unix, the computer operating system project invites users to collaborate and build upon each other's developments by copying, studying, modifying, and sharing. According to Stallman in the GNU manifesto, "Software sellers want to divide the users and conquer them, making each user agree not to share with others. I refuse to break solidarity with other users in this way." Two years after announcing the GNU project, he founded the Free Software Foundation (FSF), a donor-based organization headquartered in Boston, Massachusetts. The GNU operating system itself was completed in 1992; contributing software developer Linus Torvalds wrote its central component, which is known as the Linux kernel.

Stallman is credited with jumpstarting the free software movement, and his activism helped give rise to "copyleft." The GNU Project's Web site defines the concept as "a general method for making a program or other work free, and requiring all modified and extended versions of the program to be free as well." Although original works can simply be placed in the public domain to be free to everyone, copyleft serves a specific purpose. If software is in the public domain, a user can make slight changes and distribute the modified product with restrictions as a proprietor. On the other hand, "copyleft says that anyone who redistributes the software, with or without changes, must pass along the freedom to further copy and change it," the Web site maintains. "Copyleft guarantees that every user has freedom." The GNU project is copyleft-protected under the GNU General Public License (GPL).

Copyleft can be strong or weak, full or partial. For instance, a product derived from copyleft software may be governed by weaker or partial copyleft provisions. Copyleft is not the absence of copyright, however. Stallman maintains that "proprietary software developers use copyright to take away the users' freedom; we use copyright to guarantee their freedom." Supporters also assert that copyleft fosters innovation that may be only possible through free and public collaboration. Philosopher David M. Berry and Marcus McCallion, art director for a copyleft music label, contend, "It opens up a space of freedom and creativity for others to draw and build on your work, and for you to do likewise with theirs. This could have the potential to produce far-reaching consequences for collaboration and creativity."

Nevertheless, there is a stark difference between the free software movement and the open-source movement, wherein source codes are available to the public for collaboration and development. Accordingly, Stallman declares:

> For the free software movement, free software is an ethical imperative, because only free software respects the users'

freedom. By contrast, the philosophy of open source considers issues in terms of how to make software "better"—in a practical sense only. It says that non-free software is a suboptimal solution. For the free software movement, however, non-free software is a social problem, and moving to free software is the solution.

The open-source movement was helmed by computer programmers Bruce Perens and Eric S. Raymond, who founded the Open Source Initiative (OSI) in 1998. Although rooted in much of the same history and culture, its proponents are skeptical of the free software movement and its views. For instance, Lawrence Rosen, general counsel and secretary of OSI, rejects copyleft: "I find the word reciprocity to be less alarming and more descriptive than the word copyleft. I particularly like that word ["reciprocity"] because it does not carry with it the reference to restrictions espoused by the Free Software Foundation." As a consequence, critics insist that copyleft licensing is saddled with the same problems that afflict copyright licensing. Technology journalist Michael Fitzgerald says, "The problem is that the copyleft licenses, like the 'free software' licenses from which they're drawn, require that derivative works be licensed under identical terms. . . . So the collections (or 'mash-ups') of free text, audio, and video that [copyleft advocates] have championed as the vanguard of a new 'free culture' can't combine works created under different licenses—even if all of the licenses are meant to encourage wide sharing."

The birth of copyleft represents some of the issues of copyright laws. Defenders of copyright argue that creators of original works—recording artists, designers, programmers, and brands—need protection from infringement, piracy, and counterfeiting. On the contrary, opponents proclaim that such laws hinder innovation by stifling creativity and technological advancement. *Opposing Viewpoints: Copyright Infringement* probes this and other debates in the following chapters: What

Is Copyright Infringement? What Facilitates Copyright Infringement? What Are the Effects of Copyright Infringement? and Are Copyright Laws Effective? The authors' wide-ranging criticisms, assertions, and insights reflect the complexities of copyright laws and infringement.

CHAPTER 1

What Is Copyright Infringement?

Chapter Preface

In April 2006, Harvard sophomore Kaavya Viswanathan was accused of plagiarism in her promising debut novel, *How Opal Mehta Got Kissed, Got Wild, and Got a Life*. Viswanathan allegedly copied passages from Megan McCafferty's *Sloppy Firsts* and *Second Helpings* as well as works by Megan Cabot and Salman Rushdie. In the wake of these accusations, the offending edition of *How Opal Mehta Got Kissed* was recalled by its publisher Little, Brown and Company, and a movie deal with DreamWorks went up in smoke. In an official statement, Viswanathan apologized, claiming, "While the central stories of my book and hers are completely different, I wasn't aware of how much I may have internalized Ms. McCafferty's words. I am a huge fan of her work and can honestly say that any phrasing similarities between her works and mine were completely unintentional and unconscious." However, Random House, McCafferty's publisher, had harsh words for the first-time novelist: "This extensive taking from Ms. McCafferty's books is nothing less than an act of literary identity theft. Based on the scope and character of the similarities, it is inconceivable that this was a display of youthful innocence or an unconscious or unintentional act."

Merriam-Webster defines the verb plagiarize as "to steal and pass off (the ideas or words of another) as one's own," and while plagiarism is different from copyright infringement, legal consequences do exist. According to Tulane University law professor Glynn Lunney, allegations of copying and literary theft can be determined as infringing under the Copyright Act of 1976, and the penalties can be hundreds of thousands of dollars. "Most publishing contracts have a clause where the purported author of the work promises it's their work," Lunney maintains. Nonetheless, the similarities must be cohesive and especially striking. "If something's written in a very factual, very stripped-down way, the words might not even be copyrightable," suggests Rochelle Dreyfuss, who teaches law at New York University.

When it comes to plagiarizing, determining copyright infringement can entangle defendants and plaintiffs in a legal web. In the following chapter, authors discuss how original works are protected, how they may be legally used, and what acts constitute copyright infringement.

> *"The way in which copyright protection*
> *is secured is frequently misunderstood."*

Copyright: An Overview

Copyright Clearance Center

In the following viewpoint, Copyright Clearance Center (CCC) defines copyright as government protection provided to creators of original literary, dramatic, musical, artistic, and certain other intellectual works, such as books, sound recordings, and computer software. However, according to CCC, works not written, recorded, or captured electronically are not protected, and familiar symbols and self-evident facts (e.g., calendars, measurements) belong to the public domain. The article explains how copyright infringement occurs when permission of the copyright owner is not obtained, and discusses the complicated concept of "fair use." Founded in 1978, CCC is a nonprofit licensing and permissions organization based in Danvers, Massachusetts.

As you read, consider the following questions:

1. According to CCC, when does copyright occur?
2. What does CCC claim to be the four main categories of public domain materials?
3. How does the CCC define fair use?

Copyright Clearance Center, "Copyright Basics," 2008. Copyright © 2008 Copyright Clearance Center. Reproduced by permission of Copyright Clearance Center, Inc.

Information is everything. It points the way to advances in science and medicine, innovations in business and technology and achievements in education and the arts. The cost of research, writing and editing is substantial and the efforts often Herculean. Some books are the result of years of individual effort; others are the product of ground-breaking collaboration. Either way, without the protections guaranteed by our copyright laws, many of the works we enjoy and rely upon today would never exist.

What Is Copyright?

Much of the information in this section was drawn from content posted on the Web site of the U.S. Copyright Office and is based on the U.S. Copyright Act of 1976. The information appears here in an edited form. For the complete, unedited text visit: www.copyright.gov.

In the United States, copyright is a form of protection provided by the government to the authors of "original works of authorship, including literary, dramatic, musical, artistic, and certain other intellectual works." This protection is available to both published and unpublished works, regardless of the nationality or domicile of the author. It is unlawful for anyone to violate any of the rights provided by copyright law to the owner of the copyright.

When Copyright Occurs

Copyright protection exists from the time the work is created in a fixed, tangible form of expression. The copyright in the work of authorship *immediately* becomes the property of the author who created the work. Only the author, or those deriving their rights through the author, can rightfully claim copyright. In the case of works made for hire, the employer, not the writer, is considered to be the author.

It is important to note that mere ownership or possession of a book, manuscript, painting, etc., does not give you the copyright to the work. The law provides that transfer of ownership of any material object that embodies a protected work does not, of itself, convey any rights in the copyright. It is also important to note that including attribution on a copied work (for example, putting the author's name on it) will not relieve you from a copyright infringement claim. If the work is protected by copyright, you must obtain permission from the copyright holder to reuse it.

Registration and Other Requirements

The way in which copyright protection is secured is frequently misunderstood. Copyright is secured *automatically* when the work is created, and a work is "created" when it is fixed in a tangible form, such as the first time it is written or recorded. Neither publication, registration or other action in the Copyright Office is required to secure copyright, although registration is recommended.

The use of a copyright notice is no longer required under U.S. law, although it is often beneficial. This requirement was eliminated when the United States adhered to the Berne Convention [an agreement of 164 countries to respect each others' copyright laws], effective March 1, 1989. Should the copyright holder elect to utilize a copyright notice, he/she may do so freely without permission from or registration with the U.S. Copyright Office. In fact, the use of a copyright notice is recommended as it reminds the public that the work is protected by copyright.

The notice for visually perceptible copies should contain all the following three elements:

1. The symbol © (the letter C in a circle), or the word "Copyright," or the abbreviation "Copr."
2. The year of first publication of the work.
3. The name of the owner of copyright in the work. Example: © 2004 John Doe

Duration of Copyright

The term of copyright protection varies with the date of creation. A work created on or after January 1, 1978, is automatically protected from the moment of its creation and is ordinarily given a term enduring for the author's life plus an additional 70 years after the author's death.

For works made for hire, anonymous works and pseudonymous works (unless the author's identity is revealed in Copyright Office records), the duration of copyright will be 95 years from publication or 120 years from creation, whichever is shorter.

For works originally created and published or registered before January 1, 1978, or for more detailed information, you may wish to refer to the public domain (link) section or request Circular 15, "Renewal of Copyright;" Circular 15a, "Duration of Copyright;" and Circular 15t, "Extension of Copyright Terms," from the U.S. Copyright office, www. copyright.gov.

Public Domain

The legal concept of the public domain as it applies to copyright law should not be confused with the fact that a work may be publicly available, such as information found in books or periodicals, or on the Internet. The public domain comprises all those works that are either no longer protected by copyright or never were.

Essentially, all works first published in the United States prior to 1923 are considered to be in the public domain in the United States, as are works published between 1923 and 1963 on which copyright registrations were not renewed. Materials created since 1989, other than those created by the U.S. federal government, are presumptively protected by copyright. Therefore, the likelihood that materials of greatest interest are in the public domain is low. In addition, you must also consider other forms of legal protection, such as trademark or patent protection, before reusing third-party content.

Public domain materials generally fall into one of four categories:

1. Generic information, such as facts, numbers and ideas.

2. Works whose copyrights have lapsed due to the passage of time or the failure of the copyright holder to renew a registration (a requirement that applies to works created before 1978).

3. Works created prior to March 1989 that failed to include a proper notice of copyright.

4. Works created by the U.S. federal government. Also, in rare instances, works may be "dedicated" (donated) to the public domain.

Fair Use

The concept of fair use can be confusing and difficult to apply to particular uses of copyright protected material. Understanding the concept of fair use and when it applies may help ensure your compliance with copyright law.

Fair use is a uniquely U.S. concept, created by judges and enshrined in the law. Fair use recognizes that certain types of use of other people's copyright protected works do not require the copyright holder's authorization. In these instances, it is presumed the use is minimal enough that it does not interfere with the copyright holder's exclusive rights to reproduce and otherwise reuse the work.

Fair use is primarily designed to allow the use of the copyright protected work for commentary, parody, news reporting, research and education. However, fair use is not an exception to copyright compliance so much as it is a "legal defense."

Works Originally Created and Published or Registered Before January 1, 1978

Under the law in effect before 1978, copyright was secured either on the date a work was published with a copyright notice or on the date of registration if the work was registered in unpublished form. In either case, the copyright endured for a first term of 28 years from the date it was secured. During the last (28th) year of the first term, the copyright was eligible for renewal. The Copyright Act of 1976 extended the renewal term from 28 to 47 years for copyrights that were subsisting on January 1, 1978, or for pre-1978 copyrights restored under the Uruguay Round Agreements Act (URAA), making these works eligible for a total term of protection of 75 years. Public Law 105-298, enacted on October 27, 1998, further extended the renewal term of copyrights still subsisting on that date by an additional 20 years, providing for a renewal term of 67 years and a total term of protection of 95 years.

Public Law 102-307, enacted on June 26, 1992, amended the 1976 Copyright Act to provide for automatic renewal of the term of copyrights secured between January 1, 1964, and December 31, 1977. Although the renewal term is automatically provided, the Copyright Office does not issue a renewal certificate for these works unless a renewal application and fee are received and registered in the Copyright Office.

Public Law 102-307 makes renewal registration optional. . . . However, some benefits accrue to renewal registrations that were made during the 28th year.

U.S. Copyright Office,
"Copyright Office Basics," www.copyright.gov.

That is, if you use a copyright protected work and the copyright owner claims copyright infringement, you may be able to assert a defense of fair use, which you would then have to prove.

Section 107 of the United States Copyright Act lists four factors to help judges determine, and therefore to help you predict, when content usage may be considered "fair use."

1. *The purpose and character of the use, including whether such use is of a commercial nature or is for nonprofit, educational purposes.*

   If a particular usage is intended to help you or your organization to derive financial or other business-related benefits from the copyright material, then that is probably not fair use.

2. *The nature of the copyrighted work.*

   Use of a purely factual work is more likely to be considered fair use than use of someone's creative work.

3. *The amount and substantiality of the portion used in relation to the copyright protected work as a whole.*

   There are no set page counts or percentages that define the boundaries of fair use. Courts exercise common-sense judgment about whether what is being used is too much of, or so important to, the original overall work as to be beyond the scope of fair use.

4. *The effect of the use on the potential market for or value of the copyright protected work.*

   This factor looks at whether the nature of the use competes with or diminishes the potential market for the form of use that the copyright holder is already employing, or can reasonably be expected soon to employ, in order to make money for itself through licensing.

At one extreme, simple reproduction of a work (i.e., photocopying) is commonly licensed by copyright holders, and therefore photocopying in a business environment is not likely to be considered fair use.

At the other extreme, true parody is more likely to be considered fair use because it is unlikely that the original copyright holder would create a parody of his or her own work.

While the factors above are helpful guides, they do not clearly identify uses that are or are not fair use. Fair use is not a straightforward concept, therefore the fair use analysis must be conducted on a case-by-case basis.

Understanding the scope of fair use and becoming familiar with those situations where it applies and those where it does not can help protect you and your organization from unauthorized use of copyright materials, however, many individuals do not want this responsibility. [Corporate copyright policies] often provide guidelines for determining whether a use may be considered fair use. Frequently, a complete risk analysis is required. Most organizations prefer to follow the motto "when in doubt, obtain permission."

Thousands of cases, and many, many books and articles have attempted to analyze fair use in order to define specific examples.

Examples of Fair Use include:

- Quotation of excerpts in a review or criticism for purposes of illustration or comment.

- Quotation of short passages in a scholarly or technical work for illustration or clarification of the author's observations.

- Reproduction of material for classroom use where the reproduction was unexpected and spontaneous—for example, where an article in the morning's paper is directly relevant to that day's class topic.

- Use in a parody of short portions of the work itself.

- A summary of an address or article, which may include quotations of short passages of the copyrighted work.

The First Sale Doctrine

The physical ownership of an item, such as a book or a CD, is not the same as owning the copyright to the work embodied in that item.

Under the first sale doctrine (section 109 of the Copyright Act), ownership of a physical copy of a copyright-protected work permits lending, reselling, disposing, etc. of the item, but it does not permit reproducing the material, publicly displaying or performing it, or otherwise engaging in any of the acts reserved for the copyright holder, because the transfer of the physical copy does not include transfer of the copyright rights to the work.

Infringing Copyright

In utilizing any of the exclusive rights provided to the copyright holder without his permission, you may be violating or infringing on his rights under the Copyright Act. If the copyright holder has registered the infringed work with the U.S. Copyright Office prior to the infringement, the copyright holder may be entitled to compensation for his loss. Compensation may include damages, such as lost profits from the infringing activity, or statutory damages ranging from $250 to $150,000 for each infringing copy or higher if the court feels that the infringement was committed "willfully."

You may also be criminally liable if you willfully copy a work for profit or financial gain, or if the work has a value of more than $1,000. Penalties can include a one year jail sentence plus fines. If the value is more than $2,500, you may be sentenced to five years in jail plus fines. Criminal penalties generally apply to large-scale commercial piracy.

"International" Copyright

There is no such thing as an "international copyright" that automatically protects a work throughout the world although more than 150 countries have ratified a treaty intended to accomplish as many of the benefits of "international copyright" as possible. Generally, if a work is protected in the U.S. it is protected in most countries because the U.S. adheres to the leading copyright convention, the *Berne Convention*, which is administered by the World Intellectual Property Organisation (WIPO).

Copyright and Academia

The Copyright Act generally applies to the creation, protection and use of literary, cinematic, pictorial and many other forms of creative materials. In addition, there are some specific provisions in the Copyright Act for the use of copyright-protected materials by academic institutions, including:

- Section 107 on fair use, which applies to activities such as using excerpts for illustration or comment, unexpected and spontaneous reproduction of classroom materials, and creation of parodies.

- Section 108 on reproduction by libraries and archives, which applies to such activities as archiving; replacing lost, damaged or obsolete copies; patron requests for entire works; and interlibrary loans.

- Section 109 on first sale, which permits the resale or lending of copies of works, providing the basis for library lending and the sale of used books.

- Section 110 on performance and display in the classroom, which permits certain types of content use in the classroom and in distance education.

What Is Copyright-Protected?

Copyright-Protected	Not Copyright-Protected
Literary works	Works that have not been fixed in a tangible form of expression; written, recorded or captured electronically.
Musical works, including any accompanying words	Titles, names, short phrases and slogans; familiar symbols or designs; mere variations of typographic ornamentation, lettering or coloring; mere listings of ingredients or contents.
Dramatic works, including any accompanying music	Ideas, procedures, methods, systems, processes, concepts, principles, discoveries or devices, as distinguished from a description, explanation or illustration.
Pantomimes and choreographic works	Works consisting entirely of information that are natural or self-evident facts, containing no original authorship, such as the white pages of telephone books, standard calendars, height and weight charts and tape measures and rulers.
Pictorial, graphic and sculptural works	Works created by the U.S. Government.
Motion pictures and other audiovisual works	Works for which copyright has expired; works in the public domain.
Sound recordings	
Architectural works	
Computer Software	

"One of the biggest misconceptions about plagiarism is that it is synonymous with copyright infringement."

Plagiarism Is Different from Copyright Infringement

K. Matthew Dames

In the following viewpoint, K. Matthew Dames maintains that plagiarism and copyright infringement are distinct concepts. The author claims that copyright is governed by the principles of fair use and licensing or permissions. Plagiarism, however, is the act of passing off another creator's ideas or words without credit and does not allow exceptions, argues Dames. Furthermore, he contends that, unlike copyright infringement, which requires registration of the work and proof of violation, there are no safeguards or standards against an allegation of plagiarism, making it virtually impossible to defend. Dames is executive editor of Copysense, *an online publication, and teaches copyright and licensing at Syracuse University's School of Information Studies.*

As you read, consider the following questions:

1. What examples of plagiarism does Dames provide?

K. Matthew Dames, "Understanding Plagiarism and How It Differs from Copyright Infringement," *Computers in Libraries*, vol. 27, no. 6, June 2004, pp. 24(4). Copyright © 2004 Information Today, Inc. Reproduced by permission.

2. What "potential intersect" exists between plagiarism and copyright, according to Dames?

3. In the author's view, how can plagiarism allegations be avoided?

Ohio University, the oldest public university in the state of Ohio, is an institution with an enrollment of about 20,000 students. [In 2007], the university has been besieged by a crippling plagiarism scandal. Based on an alumnus' allegations that more than 30 students in the school's mechanical engineering department have plagiarized substantial or core portions of their graduate theses, the Athens, Ohio, institution has ordered those students to address the allegations or risk having their degrees revoked. Some of these theses are 20 years old, according to an article about the case in *The Wall Street Journal* (*WSJ*) on Aug. 15, 2006.

This front-page story was the latest in a series of plagiarism stories that seem to be destined for headline news. According to a *WSJ* article published on May 14, 2006, the board of directors at defense contractor Raytheon Co. decided it would withhold a salary increase and reduce incentive stock compensation to CEO [chief executive officer] William Swanson after it was revealed that Swanson's *Unwritten Rules of Management*, a booklet he authored, contained almost verbatim passages from *The Unwritten Rules of Engineering*, a 1944 book by W. J. King.

A few weeks earlier, publisher Little, Brown and Co. took the extraordinary step of removing the novel *How Opal Mehta Got Kissed, Got Wild, and Got a Life* from retail shelves after *The Harvard Crimson* published a story accusing author Kaavya Viswanathan, a Harvard undergraduate student, of pilfering significant portions of two teen novels written by Megan McCafferty, according to a *WSJ* article published on April 28 [2006].

Based on these developments, plagiarism has become the new piracy. Just as piracy was a few years ago, plagiarism has become the hot, new crime du jour—an act that suggests immorality and often scandal at once. What's more, plagiarism allegations feed into our society's Candid Camera mentality—our seemingly insatiable need to uncover wrongdoing. So that's why I wanted to compare plagiarism and copyright, and to write about the role of information professionals in raising the collective level of citation savvy.

Copyright Not Equal to Plagiarism

One of the biggest misconceptions about plagiarism is that it is synonymous with copyright infringement. Each passing year, I spend more time during my copyright seminar at Syracuse University explaining the distinction between (and possible intersecting points of) copyright and plagiarism.

Here's how I compare and contrast these two concepts: Copyright simply is a set of laws that governs the creation, reproduction, and distribution of original works that can be perceived. Copyright law is codified as a federal statute at Title 17 of U.S. Code [federal laws of the United States]. The most important things to remember about copyright are that 1) it is a set of laws and 2) allegations of wrongdoing—the illegal use of protected works without exception, license, or purchase—are made within the context of a standardized legal process. But more about this process later.

Plagiarism, in comparison, is the act of stealing and passing off someone else's ideas or words as one's own without crediting the source, as defined in [dictionary] *Merriam-Webster Online*. Brief or attributed quotes generally do not constitute plagiarism. Typically, no law governs plagiarism, so no one can be sued for plagiarism. Ultimately, plagiarism is about idea theft: A person tries to take an idea and claim it as his or her own.

There is also a potential intersection between plagiarism and copyright. For example, an idea can be plagiarized, but an idea cannot be copyrighted. However, if that idea is committed to paper (or otherwise recorded), then the idea can be both plagiarized and infringed. So let's take this a step further: While a recorded idea can be subject to plagiarism and copyright infringement, a person could use a recorded idea if that use falls under one or more copyright exceptions. Qualifying for one of the exceptions may remove the copyright infringement risk, but it may not necessarily remove the plagiarism risk.

In fact, a person who adds some level of ironic twist to the use may be considered a parodist and make that parody his own new, unique work that is subject to its own copyright protection. Or, given our working definition of plagiarism—the act of stealing and passing off another's ideas or words as one's own without crediting the source—one could reasonably argue that the act of parody constitutes a form of plagiarism. In many parodies, the source of the parody is instantly recognized, but does instant recognition equate to attribution?

In the end, though, copyright infringement and plagiarism are distinct and separate. But it is easier now to recognize how these concepts can get twisted.

Plagiarism Allegations

Even though copyright infringement can result in financial damages or even jail time, plagiarism allegations can be much more damaging to a person's professional reputation than allegations of copyright infringement. To support this statement, let's return to the Copyright Act. The act operates in a way that excuses infringement allegations. For example, fair use under Section 107 excuses an allegation of copyright infringement. Practically speaking, a judge may look at the facts of a case and determine that a party has actually made fair use of a work. Alternatively, a judge could determine that an accused's claim of a fair use excuse is errant. (The publishing

Exceptions to Copying Works

In the present day, the numerous cultures, disciplines and professions vary in their acceptance of copying the works of another without acknowledging the source. These differing views are based on how the individual is defined in a society or group and the accepted means by which that society or group transfers information. In the European-American culture, the self is a separate and distinct entity which redefines itself through communication of ideas. . . . Individual contributions are the measure of a person's worth. When viewed this way, taking the product of another's work diminishes the worth of the originator. When discovered, amends must be made to rectify the loss. Simple acknowledgment of the source, or financial restitution, provides the compensation.

There are exceptions to this concept within the Anglo-European culture. These exceptions derive from an agreement between the author or inventor and the one receiving recognition. Institutions and corporations, for example, may put emphasis on a product rather than the individuals who created it. . . . Politicians have speech-writers on staff to write persuasive words for various audiences. [As Richard A. Posner notes:] "Thomas Jefferson penned George Washington's Farewell Address. . . . Theodore Sorenson wrote John F. Kennedy's Pulitzer Prize–winning book, *Profiles in Courage.*" In these situations, the self has relinquished personal identity. Such an agreement between the author and the presenter subordinates the originator's need for recognition to the needs of the requester.

Judy Anderson, Plagiarism, Copyright, and Other Thefts of Intellectual Property, *1998.*

industry has been making just such an argument in its lawsuit over Google Book Search.) [1] But in the end, copyright law allows for the possibility that allegedly illegal conduct may be excusable or defensible.

Federal copyright law (along with federal rules of evidence and civil litigation procedure) also typically places certain burdens on the accuser, including the burden of proving that an infringement occurred and that the accused is the party responsible for the infringement. Copyright law also imposes prerequisites that must be met even before an accuser makes an allegation: Pursuant to Section 411, a copyright owner cannot start a copyright infringement lawsuit unless the work at issue is registered with the Copyright Office in Washington, D.C. Given the excuses available to the accused, the procedural safeguards, and evidentiary safeguards, it is easy to see how the copyright system tries to balance the rights and reputations of the accused and the accuser.

Plagiarism allegations, however, have no such safeguards. Allegations of plagiarism do not require registration, and they do not require that the accuser prove the allegation. Plagiarism allegations do not even require that the injured party be the one who alleges wrongdoing. In most cases, third parties identify potential acts of plagiarism, make public allegations, then let the public rumor mill consider the facts. The accuser is never called upon to account for the veracity or falsity of his claim.

Plagiarism cases may involve an accuser's questionable motives. For example, the person alleging plagiarism in the Ohio University case is an alumnus who was initially unable to get his thesis topic approved, according to the *WSJ* article. The article fails to ask (or answer) what seems to be an obvious question: Did the accuser have a big enough grudge against the students who graduated before him to discredit

1. Google Book Search is a project to digitize libary books, making them available online. The suit was settled in October 2008.

their work? While no proof exists that the accuser in the Ohio University scandal was fueled by such a motive, it is still a legitimate question.

Further, the *WSJ* report does not identify any conclusive determination that any of the alleged plagiarizers intentionally used another person's content with the intent to deceive the reader that such content (or the ideas therein) was original. The story includes reports that seem worth investigating, but it seems the burden now lies with the accused to prove the claim effectively: They did not plagiarize. That is a tough position to be in.

What's more, plagiarism claims inherently presume that the accused has a guilty mind: The alleged plagiarist intentionally and knowingly copied and failed to attribute another person's work. But in many well-known plagiarism cases, the accused deny any intent to fail to attribute. Some say it is industrial sloppiness. This may or may not be true, but if industrial sloppiness—not stealth—is the real reason for not attributing something, then that seems different than an instance where a person's mens rea [criminal intent] is such that he meant to cheat. Certainly, the former does not seem to warrant destruction of the accused's professional reputation.

(As an aside, an issue that seems to be lost within these discussions is the failure of educational institutions—domestic and international, at all levels—to train students properly for the rigors of high-level academic work, including technical writing and citation. That subject should be addressed elsewhere.)

The lack of standards in plagiarism cases make an accusation virtually impossible to defend, but the mere allegation of plagiarism is considered an often irreversible smudge against a person's professional and personal values and ethics. This modern version of the scarlet letter points to one of the biggest problems with plagiarism: Without any clear standard, no burden of proof, and virtually no defenses, mere accusations of plagiarism can crush reputations faster than any allegation of copyright infringement.

Potential Plagiarism Solutions

This plagiarism controversy will not end any time soon. Interestingly, information professionals can play a role in helping knowledge workers with academic and technical writing. From a reference standpoint, several academic and corporate libraries will have subject matter specialists to help sift through and manage the literature on a given topic. The best librarians also will be quite familiar with standard citation conventions in that literature, and perhaps even will have available citation style guides that distill citation intricacies into manageable and repeatable steps.

Some libraries are even going further by providing access to Web-based citation management software. These service offerings are consistent with the contemporary trend of moving applications off the desktop, and instead, leveraging the Web as a computing platform. The benefit to packages such as RefWorks is that the citations are centrally located and organized, and accessible from a reliable Web connection. Many of these packages also interface both with online databases and with Voyager-based library systems [Voyager is a widely used library computer platform]. This integration lets you drop citations right into the software from articles and catalog records.

Plagiarism accusations can dog and derail professional careers, even of those who have made legitimate or honest errors. The best way to stay out of plagiarism's bright, unflattering spotlight is to identify citation customs (these will differ according to industry), learn those customs and citation standards, and, where possible, seek training or assistance in mastering and applying those standards.

> "There is nothing in our legal frame-
> work that has ever conceived of "fair
> use" being a defense to individuals dis-
> tributing copyrighted music for free to
> millions of people worldwide."

Online Music Piracy Is Copyright Infringement

Matthew J. Oppenheim

In the following viewpoint, Matthew J. Oppenheim argues that downloading and uploading music on peer-to-peer (P2P) networks is large-scale copyright infringement. He contends that P2P businesses reap profit from the work of artists, songwriters, and musicians, yet do not invest in artist promotion or development. Along with these businesses, he cautions that individuals who copy or distribute music on these networks could face criminal and civil liability. Oppenheim is former senior vice president for legal and business affairs of the Recording Institute Association of America (RIAA), the trade group that represents the U.S. recording industry.

As you read, consider the following questions:

1. In Oppenheim's view, why have music sales dramatically declined?

Matthew J. Oppenheim, California Senate Testimony: Testimony of Matthew J. Oppenheim, March 27, 2003. www.riaa.org. Reproduced by permission.

2. How does the P2P business model differ from the record company model, in the author's opinion?

3. What alternative to pirating music on P2P networks does the author suggest?

Senator [Kevin] Murray and Members of the Committee. Let me say in advance of my remarks that I appreciate the opportunity to appear here today on behalf of the Recording Industry to discuss music piracy on peer-to-peer networks. It is without a doubt the most important issue affecting the music industry today. Music piracy does not distinguish among artist, songwriter, publisher, record store employee, CD plant worker or record label. Its impact is widespread.

[From 2000 to 2003], the recording industry has seen dramatic declines in its sales. [In 2002], sales were down approximately 11 percent. In 2001, sales declined approximately 10 percent. And, in 2000, sales went down seven percent. For an industry that has seen stable growth for many years, this sudden and dramatic decline is having, and will continue to have, severe consequences for the industry. These consequences include music industry employees being laid off, a decrease in funding to find new artists and market new releases to consumers, and [are] generally negatively impacting the U.S. economy as a whole. While in the past some people questioned why the decline was occurring, it is now undisputed that this decline is in large part a result of the unrelenting piracy occurring on P2P [peer-to-peer] networks.

While there are a number of P2P networks, the predominant ones are the FastTrack and Gnutella networks. The Fast-Track network is supplied and maintained by Kazaa, which is now run by Sharman Networks, Grokster and Imesh. The Gnutella network is supplied and maintained predominately by Morpheus, which is run by MusicCity, Limewire and Bearshare. To quote Judge Aspen of the Northern District of Illinois from his decision about another P2P system, the "raison d'etre of [these companies] is copyright infringement."

Off of the Backs of Others

Kazaa and these other P2P companies have been successful in at least two respects: first, they have a very large and growing population of users. At last count, there were approximately 4.5 million users on the FastTrack network at any given moment, and those users were distributing over 880 million different files. These numbers are growing at a rapid pace. Second, and maybe more importantly from their perspective, they are doing something that many record companies are not doing right now: they are earning a lot of money. A *Los Angeles Times* article from May, 2002, reported that Kazaa and Morpheus are collecting more than $450,000 per month from advertising alone. Given the explosive growth of the network since that time, one can only assume that the true numbers are significantly higher now.

All of this success should come as no surprise. These companies are building businesses off of the backs of others. They pay nothing to the creators—the songwriters, artists, or back-up musicians—of the music that is driving their business. They invest nothing in the marketing and promotion of the music, and they take no risks in supporting new and developing artists. Without leeching from others, P2P businesses could not exist.

Legally, the strong and clear precedents in both the Napster and Aimster cases [two early popular file-sharing companies, both of which restructured after court decisions against them] make clear that these types of P2P businesses are liable for both contributory and vicarious copyright infringement occurring on their networks and they will be held to be financially responsible for the massive harm they are causing. In both of those cases, federal courts enjoined the P2P companies from participating in the illegal distribution of copyrighted music.

As many know, the music and movie industries have filed suit in federal court against Kazaa, Grokster, MusicCity and

Sharman Networks, among others. Those suits are currently moving forward, despite the efforts of Sharman Networks, the purveyor of Kazaa, to claim that its incorporation on the tiny island of Vanuatu in the Pacific Ocean exempted it from being held accountable in a U.S. Court. They made this claim notwithstanding the fact that the vast majority of its profits are coming from the United States, and that virtually all of its software distribution occurs through [software vendor] CNET—in the United States.

I will not take time now to review information that was the subject of Congressional hearings in Washington [in early 2003], but I would recommend that the committee consider the report released by the General Accounting Office in February, 2003 that concluded that: "It is easy to access and download child pornography on peer to peer networks. Juvenile users of peer to peer networks also face a significant risk of inadvertent exposure to pornography, including child pornography." Obviously, the fact that these P2P networks may be one of the largest sources of child pornography in the world is a serious issue that far exceeds the issues raised by the copyright community.

"Fair Use"

In their defense, the P2P companies constantly sing the same refrain about the "non-infringing uses" of the system and "fair use."

Evidence shows that 90 percent of the works distributed on the FastTrack network is infringing. This fact is not surprising, and is entirely consistent with studies of other similar pirate havens. In the well-known Napster case, it was shown that fully 87 percent of the music on that network was infringing material. Additionally, in a study released last week by [information security company] Palisade Systems, it was determined that 99 percent of the audio files sought on the Gnutella network were copyrighted. These statistical studies

One in Three

Some people mistakenly think that all piracy these days takes place on the internet. That is very far from the truth. It is true that in some countries, like Taiwan and Korea, internet piracy has replaced not just legitimate business but also physical piracy. However, fighting piracy of physical CDs and DVDs is just as great a priority to our industry today as it ever was. The market in illegal music sales is around 4 billion euros—one eighth of the value of the global music market—and that is only at the low prices that pirates charge. [From 2000 to 2005] the number of pirate discs has doubled to more than 1 billion discs sold—that means that one in three of all music CDs sold worldwide is an illegal copy.

John Kennedy, "Giving Music a Chance:
Promoting New Markets and Fighting Piracy,"
IFPI, May 26, 2005. www.ifpi.org.

reveal what is obvious to anybody who actually uses these networks: their purpose and reason for being are infringement, or stealing.

Moreover, P2P companies seem to think "fair use" means "free use." But there is nothing in our legal framework that has ever conceived of "fair use" being a defense to individuals distributing copyrighted music for free to millions of people worldwide. P2P companies talk about "file-sharing," but there is nothing about this that involves "sharing." When I share one of my CDs with a friend, I give my CD to my friend. I no longer have it. With these P2P networks, "sharing" means that I keep the original and give someone a perfect digital copy. "Sharing" in the P2P world is a euphemism for stealing. The poignant truth demonstrates that the unauthorized P2P networks are nothing more than piracy bazaars.

And like the piracy bazaars of ancient times, these piracy bazaars are equally dangerous for the unknowing. Most P2P users accidentally end up opening personal files on their computers to strangers that they have no intention of sharing. Sometimes the files are innocuous documents, but more often than not it is financial data, credit card information or tax returns. A Hewlett-Packard [report] of June of 2002 concluded: "a large number of users are currently sharing personal and private files without their knowledge, and . . . that other users are indeed taking advantage of this and downloading files such as 'Credit Cards.xls' and e-mail files."

Not only are individuals unknowingly sharing personal information, P2P companies are surreptitiously taking personal information from their users. Most of these companies hide in their software very dangerous applications commonly referred to as "spyware." This spyware allows unknown third party companies to secretly collect data about what users are doing on their computers.

The Most Significant Threat

But by and far, the most significant threat that individuals face from copying and distributing music, movies, software and images on these networks is the criminal and civil liability to which they expose themselves. The law in this arena is clear: downloading or uploading a copyrighted work without the explicit permission of the owner is copyright infringement. That infringement can subject the individual to prosecution under the NET [No Electronic Theft] Act, or civil suit under the Copyright Act. Under either scenario, the penalties are fierce.

The business model of the P2P companies is a stark contrast to legitimate record companies that pay artists and songwriters, market and promote their product, distribute their product through both physical and online retailers and invest in new artists. That legitimate business model however is currently at risk, as is the future of music for consumers. In order for record companies to continue releasing new music, market that music, develop new artists, and develop new formats, they must be able to have an expectation that they can recoup their investment. That expectation is now being challenged because piracy, by its nature, swoops in and steals that return.

The problem with peer to peer is not the technology, but how it is used. Peer to peer technology is exciting and has many legitimate uses. Unfortunately, the unauthorized systems discussed here today are distributing copyrighted material without the copyright owners' consent.

For all kinds of reasons, some good and some not so good, the music industry was slow in offering to consumers legitimate online alternatives to these P2P networks. Having said that, the legitimate alternatives are now out there and they rock. Whether your preference is PressPlay, Rhapsody, Listen, RioPort, FullAudio, Emusic or MusicMatch or another licensed source, you can now go online and get legitimate high quality music online in many different forms. These new services, however, face a very tough uphill battle. In addition to all of the demands of building a legitimate online business, they must compete with the free and illegal services that the P2P companies are offering.

So what should we do? One answer is that individuals need to be educated about these issues. Individuals need to know that using these networks is not without risk, and potentially very serious consequences. Along the same lines, companies need to monitor their networks to make sure that their employees are not engaging in this behavior—behavior that can expose the companies to significant problems. Finally, universities also need to be aware of these issues, know what is happening on their networks and educate their students and faculty of the potential consequences of their actions.

As our community increases its focus on these issues, and individuals become educated about these issues, the record industry is hopeful that we can continue to support the art that is so important to our country.

> *"Downloading movies . . . without the authorization of copyright holders is a growing international problem that presents serious challenges for the movie industry and has serious legal consequences."*

Movie Piracy Is Copyright Infringement

Motion Picture Association of America

In the following viewpoint, the Motion Picture Association of America (MPAA) asserts that anyone who sells, acquires, copies, distributes, or publicly broadcasts a copyrighted movie or DVD without permission infringes on copyright laws. Similarly, according to the association, a consumer engages in piracy if he or she downloads a movie illegally, buys a pirated DVD, or shares it through a peer-to-peer (P2P) network. A single digital movie can be downloaded millions of times for free; consequently, the film industry loses billions of dollars a year to the different forms of movie piracy, the MPAA contends. Founded in 1922, the Motion Picture Association of America (MPAA) is the trade association of the American film industry.

Motion Picture Association of America, "Anti-piracy: Who Are Movie Thieves?" 2005. Copyright © 2005 Motion Picture Association of America. Reproduced by permission.

As you read, consider the following questions:

1. How does the MPAA describe a P2P network?
2. Why is theatrical camcorder piracy a threat to the film industry, in the MPAA's view?
3. What other forms of movie piracy does the author describe?

Anyone who sells, acquires, copies or distributes copyrighted materials without permission is called a pirate. Downloading a movie without paying for it is no different than walking into a store and stealing a DVD off the shelf. Motion Picture Piracy is committed in many ways, including via the Internet through downloadable files, selling pirated DVDs on the street or capturing and redistributing live broadcasts or performances without a license on the Internet. Downloading movies and music without the authorization of copyright holders is a growing international problem that presents serious challenges for the movie industry and has serious legal consequences.

People often download movies on the Internet because they believe they are anonymous and will not be held responsible for their actions. They are wrong. The illegal downloading and swapping of movie files is a serious crime. Pirates and their affiliates can and will be tracked for engaging in Internet piracy.

Internet Piracy

By 2007, IDC Research expects Internet users will access, download, and share information equivalent to the contents of the entire Library of Congress more than 64,000 times every day.

What Is Internet Piracy?

Internet piracy is the downloading or distribution of unauthorized copies of intellectual property such as movies, television, music, games and software programs via the Internet. Illegal downloads occur in many forms including file sharing networks, pirate servers, websites and hacked computers. Each file posted on the Internet can result in millions of downloads. Hard goods pirates also use the Internet to sell illegally duplicated DVDs through auctions and websites. Piracy is theft, and pirates are thieves, plain and simple. Downloading a movie off of the Internet is the same as taking a DVD off a store shelf without paying for it. In 2005, MPAA studios lost $2.3 billion worldwide to Internet piracy alone. Posting movies on a peer-to-peer (P2P) service or an unauthorized website is akin to giving illegal copies to millions of people.

The Global Avalanche of Internet Piracy

The primary source of newly released pirated movies comes from thieves who camcord films in theaters. Illegally recorded movies are then sold to individuals who distribute them around the world through computer servers known as "Topsites." The extraordinary speed and power of a Topsite triggers the avalanche that is global Internet piracy. . . .

What Are Peer-to-Peer (P2P) File-Sharing Services?

A peer-to-peer service is a network that enables computers to connect directly to each other in order to distribute and copy files. Software programs utilize these networks to search for and trade every kind of file. Examples of P2P services include eDonkey, Kazaa, Limewire and DirectConnect. These programs can turn your computer into a directory and distributor of an unlimited variety of illegal material, viruses and worms.

When you download a file from the P2P services, you're not just receiving stolen goods. You're now a dealer, responsible for all the violations that others are enabled to commit as a result. Besides putting yourself at risk of the legal consequences of illegally distributing movies, you're opening your computer up to potentially dangerous situations. By inviting complete strangers to access your hard drive, you risk exposing your private information such as bank records, social security numbers and personal pictures. You also make yourself vulnerable to identity theft and possibly a whole lot more. In addition, you are exposing your computer to harmful viruses, worms, Trojan horses and annoying pop-ups.

What Is the MPAA Doing to Combat the Problem?

The MPAA [Motion Picture Association of America] has a multi-pronged approach to fighting Internet piracy, which includes educating people about the consequences of piracy, taking action against Internet thieves, working with law enforcement authorities around the world to root out pirate operations and working to ensure that advanced technologies will allow the legal distribution of movies over the Internet. Since November of 2004, individuals who have infringed copyrights in motion pictures and television programs over the Internet have been sued for those infringements in lawsuits in the smallest of towns and the biggest of cities. Damages for copyright infringement range from $30,000 to $150,000 per work and, if there is criminal prosecution, could include up to five years in jail.

Legal Alternatives

As a consumer, there are plenty of sites that offer legal downloads such as CinemaNow, Vongo, ifilm, Movielink, Movieflix, AtomFilms, iTunes video and more. You can also get show times and tickets for movies playing in local theatres online. There are also many options available to buy or rent movies without even having to leave your home. For students, services such as Cdigix and Ruckus are becoming readily available on college and university campuses across the nation.

What Is Optical Disc Piracy?

Optical disc piracy is the illegal manufacturing, sale, distribution or trading of copies of motion pictures in digital disc formats including DVD, DVD-R, CD, CD-R and VCD. These illegal hard goods are sold on websites, online auction sites, via e-mail solicitation and by street vendors and flea markets around the world. Much like downloadable media, the pirated motion pictures in hard goods format are typically poor quality video camera recordings.

While the majority of pirated optical disc products seized by law enforcement worldwide are made on advanced commercial replication lines, the low cost of disc burning hardware and blank discs has led to the proliferation of DVD-R and CD-R burner labs.

Fighting Optical Disc Piracy Around the World:

- Working with law enforcement around the world, the MPAA seized over 81 million illegal optical discs in 2005.

- According to a study conducted by LEK Consulting LLC, MPAA companies lost approximately $3.8 billion worldwide to physical piracy in 2005.

- To combat the problem, the MPA [Motion Picture Association] launched the "Tactics for Auction Piracy" (TAP) initiative, taking quick action against several people across the country that were selling a significant amount of pirated DVDs via online auction houses. It is our hope that this will not only help protect unsuspecting consumers, but also that it will send a message to those engaging in the illegal sale of movies that the motion picture industry is serious about protecting its copyrighted works.

- The MPAA/MPA directs its worldwide anti-piracy activities from headquarters in Encino, California, and conducts local activities from regional offices located in Brussels (Europe, Middle East and Africa), Sao Paolo (Latin America) and Singapore (Asia/Pacific).

Theatrical Camcorder Piracy

Ninety percent of pirated copies of movies are still playing in theaters. Once a camcorded copy is made, illegal movies often appear online within hours or days of a movie premiere. Pirates sell these "master recordings" to illicit "source labs" where they are illegally duplicated, packaged and prepared for sale on the black market, then distributed to bootleg "dealers" across the country and overseas. Consequently, the film appears in street markets around the world just days after the US theatrical release and well before its international debut. . . .

Other Piracy

Theatrical Print Theft

Theft of an actual film print (35 or 16 mm) from a theater, film depot, courier service or other industry-related facility for the purpose of making illegal copies is one of the most serious forms of piracy. This type of theft allows the pirate to make a relatively high quality videotape from the theatrical print, which then serves as the master for the duplication of unauthorized videocassettes. Fortunately, this type of theft is extremely rare due to the difficulty in obtaining the prints illegally and also in transferring the print to another format, such as videocassettes.

Signal Theft

Signal theft refers to the act of illegally tapping into cable TV systems as well as receiving satellite signals without authorization. In addition, pirates have supplied consumers with illegal cable decoders or satellite descramblers. Internationally, the problem becomes more acute when programs not licensed to a particular country are pirated from satellites and then retransmitted in that country either by cable or broadcast TV.

Broadcast Piracy

Like signal theft, broadcast piracy is piracy involving over-the-air broadcasts. However, instead of stealing signals, the illegal act may be the on-air broadcasting of films or television programs without permission from the copyright holder.

Camcorder Piracy

The most common suppliers are people who sneak a camcorder into a theater and aim it at the screen.... Movie studios have lately tried to thwart screen cams by arming movie theater attendants with metal detectors and night-vision goggles and engaging them as anti-Scene mercenaries.

The supplier passes the unreleased film to a contact in a release group or puts it on a drop site, a hidden server on the Internet. The movie is then sent to a ripper by overnight mail if it is on DVD or, if it is on a drop site, by telling the ripper to grab the file through a secure computer line called a virtual private network connection or VPN. The ripper (sometimes called a cracker) copies the movie's raw video and audio files, and he or an encoder edits out the identifying marks that studios insert to track copies. The ripper also compresses the video file into formats suitable for downloading and viewing on a computer or television screen.

Next, a distributor places a file on one of 30 or so topsites—secure digital locations that can be entered only with a password. From there, couriers transfer the file to high-speed distribution servers, computers configured to share files. Finally, the channel operators announce the movie's availability on individual IRC channels.... Forest estimates that 1,500 IRC channels are devoted exclusively to movie piracy. The entire process usually takes two to three days....

Joseph D. Lasica, "The Price of Darknet,"
Legal Affairs, May/June 2005.

Public Performance

Unauthorized public performances include situations where an institution or commercial establishment shows a tape or film to its members or customers without receiving permission from the copyright owner. This includes "public performances" where an admission fee is charged as well as those that are simply offered as an additional service of the establishment.

Parallel Imports

Parallel imports describes the importation of goods authorized for manufacture or distribution in the exporting country but imported without authority of the copyright or trademark owner. (Parallel importation may or may not be lawful under local laws).

Videocassette Piracy

Videocassette piracy is the illegal duplication, distribution, rental or sale of copyrighted videocassettes. In recent years, the MPAA/MPA shifted its investigative focus onto the illicit duplicating facilities or "laboratories" that are set-up to create and distribute pirated videocassettes. These facilities are often times capable of producing hundreds of thousands of illegal videocassette copies each year. These copies are then distributed to a variety of outlets including swap meets, co-operating video dealers and street vendors. The pirate product is often packaged in counterfeit videocassette boxes that resemble legitimate packaging.

Camcording: Pirates use hand-held video cameras to record motion picture films off of theater screens and then copy these films onto blank videocassettes and optical discs for illegal distribution. These illicit copies are not only distributed to pirates in the US, but also shipped overseas and distributed through illegal channels even before the film's international theatrical release.

Screeners: Illegal copies are sometimes made from legitimate advance copies used for screening and marketing purposes.

Back-to-back Copying: A "back-to-back" copy is a pirate videocassette made by connecting two VCRs and then copying an original video onto a blank cassette.

> *"Copying software illegally is not any different than illegally copying any of these forms of intellectual property—and the punishments for doing so are equally harsh."*

Software Piracy Is Copyright Infringement

Software & Information Industry Association

In the following viewpoint, the Software & Information Industry Association (SIIA) asserts that software is a relatively new form of intellectual property, and its unauthorized use, duplication, or distribution is copyright infringement. The association contends that people ignorantly or deliberately engage in software piracy, including "sharing" it or installing the software on unauthorized machines, while software pirates sell their illegal wares on online auctions and at computer shows. According to the SIIA, the resulting revenue losses set back software research and development; also, software piracy exposes end users—from individuals to entire companies—to software vulnerabilities and penalties for copyright infringement. The SIIA is a trade association of the software and digital content industries.

Software & Information Industry Association (SIIA), "What Is Piracy?" 2008. www .siia.net. Copyright © 2008 The Software & Information Industry Association. All rights reserved. Reproduced by permission.

As you read, consider the following questions:

1. In the SIIA's view, what is the scope of software piracy in the United States?
2. What is "softlifting," according to the SIIA?
3. As described by the association, how has compact disc recording (CD-R) technology affected software piracy?

Over the past several years, advances in computer software have brought us time-saving business programs, educational software that teaches basic skills and sophisticated subjects, graphics programs that have revolutionized the design industry, Internet applications that help connect us with other computer users, and an increasingly complex variety of computer games to entertain us. As the software industry grows, everyone stands to benefit.

Compared to literature, music and movies, computer software is a relatively new form of intellectual property. Nevertheless, software is protected under the very same laws that govern music, literature, movies and other copyrighted content. Copying software illegally is not any different than illegally copying any of these forms of intellectual property—and the punishments for doing so are equally harsh.

All software comes with a license agreement that specifically states the terms and conditions under which the software may be legally used. Licenses vary from program to program and may authorize as few as one computer or individual to use the software or as many as several hundred network users to share the application across the system. It is important to read and understand the license accompanying the application to ensure that you have enough legal copies of the software for your organization's needs. Making additional copies, or loading the software onto more than one machine, may violate copyright law and be considered piracy.

Unfortunately, there are many people who, either ignorantly or deliberately, engage in software piracy. Whenever you use a piece of software that is unlicensed, you are depriving software companies of their earnings. More importantly, you are depriving the creative teams who have developed the software (e.g., programmers, writers, graphic artists) of compensation for the thousands of hours they have spent working on a particular program.

In a very real sense, software piracy adversely affects the world economy by diverting money that stimulates further product development. Piracy particularly affects the United States, which currently provides approximately 80 percent of the world's software.

The Dimensions of the Piracy Problem

On average, the software industry loses about US$11 to US$12 billion in revenue to software piracy annually. Of the billions of dollars lost to piracy, a little less than half comes from Asia, where China and Indonesia are the biggest offenders. Piracy is also a big problem in Western Europe, where piracy losses annually range from $2.5 and $3 billion dollars. Piracy rates are quite high in Latin America and in Central Europe, but their software markets are so much smaller that the dollar losses are considerably lower.

About $2 billion in piracy losses come from North America. The piracy rate in the United States has been relatively constant at about 25% over the past few years, which is the lowest rate of any country. This means that one in every four copies of business application software is used illegally. The large dollar amount in losses is attributable more to the fact that there are so many computers and computer users in the United States than to a high piracy rate when compared with the rest of the world.

SIIA [Software & Information Industry Association] works with the U.S. government, foreign governments and international organizations around the world to protect intellectual property in international markets. As an example, the Special 301 provision of the Omnibus Trade and Competitiveness Act of 1988 authorizes the U.S. Trade Representative (USTR) [federal agency that negotiates trade agreements with other countries] to prepare lists of countries that do not provide effective protection of intellectual property rights or deny fair and equitable market access to U.S. firms relying on intellectual property protection. The lists inform the [U.S. government] about countries considered priority targets for future trade negotiations or possible trade sanctions. . . .

There is no evidence that software piracy will be eliminated any time in the foreseeable future. SIIA acknowledges that many countries have made efforts to improve intellectual property protection for computer software. However, the high rates of software piracy and dramatic losses to U.S. software developers demonstrate that much remains to be done. There is evidence that continuing education and enforcement efforts can—and do—make a difference. In the United States, for example, the level of piracy has been reduced from 48 percent in 1989 to 25 percent in 2002.

We have learned that reducing software piracy rates requires the combined efforts of policy-makers, software developers and publishers, businesses, journalists and concerned individuals. As long as software piracy exists, there will be fewer jobs, less research and development, increased costs and lower standards of living.

Consequences of Software Piracy

The losses suffered through software piracy directly affect the profitability of the software industry. Because of the money lost to pirates, publishers have fewer resources to devote to research and development of new products, have less revenue to justify lowering software prices and are forced to pass these costs on to their customers. Consequently, software publishers, developers, and vendors are taking serious actions to protect their revenues.

Using pirated software is also risky for users. Aside from the legal consequences of using pirated software, your organization forfeits some practical benefits as well. Those who use pirate software:

- Increase the chances that the software will not function correctly or will fail completely;

- Forfeit access to customer support, upgrades, technical documentation, training, and bug fixes;

- Have no warranty to protect themselves;

- Increase their risk of exposure to a debilitating virus that can destroy valuable data;

- May find that the software is actually an outdated version, a beta (test) version, or a nonfunctioning copy;

- Are subject to significant fines for copyright infringement; and

- Risk potential negative publicity and public and private embarrassment.

It is also worth noting that the use of pirated software also drives up the costs for legitimate users—which gives legitimate users all the more reason to help SIIA fight piracy by reporting to us those companies that are not "playing by the rules."

Types of Software Piracy

Many computer users have found themselves caught in the piracy trap, unaware they were doing anything illegal. To avoid such unpleasant surprises, it may be helpful to know the ten basic ways one can intentionally or unintentionally pirate software:

1. *Softlifting*

   Softlifting occurs when a person purchases a single licensed copy of a software program and loads it on several machines, in violation of the terms of the license
   agreement. Typical examples of softlifting include, "sharing" software with friends and co-workers and installing
   software on home/laptop computers if not allowed to do
   so by the license. In the corporate environment, softlifting is the most prevalent type of software piracy—and
   perhaps, the easiest to catch.

2. *Unrestricted Client Access*

   Unrestricted client access piracy occurs when a copy of a
   software program is copied onto an organization's servers and the organization's network "clients" are allowed
   to freely access the software in violation of the terms of
   the license agreement. This is a violation when the organization has a "single instance" license that permits installation of the software onto a single computer, rather
   than a client-server license that allows concurrent server-
   based network access to the software. A violation also
   occurs when the organization has a client-server license,
   and the organization is not enforcing user restrictions
   outlined in the license. For instance, when the license
   places a restriction on the number of concurrent users
   that are allowed access to that program and the organization is not enforcing that number. Unrestricted client
   access piracy is similar to softlifting, in that it results in
   more employees having access to a particular program
   than is permitted under the license for that software.
   Unlike softlifting though, unrestricted client access piracy occurs when the software is loaded onto a
   company's server—not on individual machines—and
   clients are permitted to access the server-based software
   application through the organization's network.

3. *Hard-disk Loading*

Hard-disk loading occurs when an individual or company sells computers preloaded with illegal copies of software. Often this is done by the vendor as an incentive to buy certain hardware. If you buy or rent computers with preloaded software, your purchase documentation and contract with the vendor must specify which software is preloaded and that these are legal, licensed copies. If it does not and the vendor is unwilling to supply you with the proper documentation, do not deal with that vendor. . . .

4. *OEM Piracy/Unbundling*

Some software, known as OEM (original equipment manufacturer) software, is only legally sold with specified hardware. When these programs are copied and sold separately from the hardware, this is a violation of the distribution contract between the vendor and the software publisher. Similarly, the term "unbundling" refers to the act of selling software separately that is legally sold only when bundled with another package. Software programs that are marked "not for resale" are often bundled applications.

5. *Commercial Use of Noncommercial Software*

Using educational or other commercial-use-restricted software in violation of the software license is a form of software piracy. Software companies will often market special noncommercial software aimed at a particular audience. For example, many software companies sell educational versions of their software to public schools, universities and other educational institutions. The price of this software is often greatly reduced by the publisher in recognition of the educational nature of the institutions. Acquiring and using noncommercial software hurts not only the software publisher, but also the institution that was the intended recipient of the software.

6. *Counterfeiting*

Counterfeiting is the duplication and sale of unauthorized copies of software in such a manner as to try to pass off the illegal copy as if it were a legitimate copy produced or authorized by the legal publisher. Much of the software offered for bargain sale at non-trade computer shows is counterfeit software. SIIA estimates that at least 50% of the software sales that take place at computer shows throughout the United States involve counterfeit software.

7. *CD-R Piracy*

CD-R [compact disc recordable] piracy is the illegal copying of software using CD-R recording technology. This form of piracy occurs when a person obtains a copy of a software program and makes a copy or copies and redistributes them to friends or for resale. Although there is some overlap between CD-R piracy and counterfeiting, with CD-R piracy there may be no attempt to try to pass off the illegal copy as a legitimate copy—it may have hand-written labels and no documentation at all. With CD recording equipment becoming relatively inexpensive, the software industry is being plagued by this new form of end-user piracy. Just a few years ago, so-called "compilation CDs" (illegal CD-ROMs containing many different software applications) were selling for $400–$500. With CD-Rs becoming more available, the price has dropped to $20—making illegal software available to a greater number of people.

8. *Internet Piracy*

Internet piracy is the uploading of commercial software (i.e., software that is not freeware or public domain) on to the Internet for anyone to copy or copying commercial software from any of these services. Internet piracy also includes making available or offering for sale pirated software over the Internet. Examples of this include the offering of software through an auction site, IM [Internet message], IRC [Internet relay chat] or a warez ["darknet" software] site. Incidences of Internet piracy have risen exponentially over the last few years. Internet piracy is discussed in greater detail below.

9. *Manufacturing Plant Sale of Overruns and 'Scraps'*

Software publishers routinely authorize CD manufacturing plants to produce copies of their software onto CD-ROM so that they can distribute these CD-ROMs to their authorized vendors for resale to the public. Plant piracy occurs when the plant produces more copies of the software than it was authorized to make, and then resells these unauthorized overruns. Piracy also occurs when the plant is ordered by the publisher to destroy any CDs not distributed to its vendors, but the plant, in violation of these orders, resells those CDs that were intended to be scrapped. While most plants appear to be compliant, and there are compliance procedures in place, there have been several instances of these forms of piracy.

10. *Renting*

Renting software for temporary use, like you would a movie, was made illegal in the United States by the Software Rental Amendments Act of 1990 and in Canada by a 1993 amendment to the Copyright Act. As a result, rental of software is rare.

The ten types of piracy identified above are not mutually exclusive. There is often overlap between one type of piracy and another. For instance, SIIA has come across numerous instances of OEM counterfeiting. This occurs when OEM soft-

Surprisingly Easy

It is surprisingly easy for a company to get caught using copied software. BSA [Business Software Alliance] receives hundreds of reports on its hotline, 1-888NOPIRACY, and on its web site, www.bsa.org. Those reports generally come from current and former employees of the infringing company.... In any event, BSA does do an initial investigation before contacting a company. In most cases, contact is made with the alleged infringing company thereby giving them a chance to cooperate. Sometimes, BSA will file a complaint requesting a motion for a temporary restraining order and a motion for seizure. Once those motions are granted, the BSA, accompanied by federal marshals, go straight to the infringing company and conduct an audit on the spot.

Laura DiBiase, "Beyond the Quill: Costly Copies,"
American Bankruptcy Institute Journal, *April 2001.*

ware is unbundled in order to be re-sold, and not only does the pirate sell the OEM software, but he also makes numerous illegal copies of the OEM software and sells them as counterfeits.

Shareware and Freeware

Many users become understandably confused between shareware, freeware and public domain software. These are all ways of marketing software, and have nothing to do with the actual type of software being distributed.

Shareware is [defined by the U.S. government as] "copyrighted software which is distributed for the purposes of testing and review, subject to the condition that payment to the copyright owner is required after a person who has secured a copy decides to use the software." ...

Freeware is software that is distributed in a way that allows individuals and non-profit organizations to use the software at no charge. The software usually comes with a license agreement that prohibits the software from being sold, rented, or otherwise distributed in a for-profit manner.

Public domain software is [defined by the U.S. government as] "software which has been publicly distributed with an explicit disclaimer of copyright protection by the copyright owner."

Lastly there is another category, often referred to as crippleware that is a hybrid between shareware and freeware. Crippleware allows a person to use the software for free. If the individual likes the software, he/she can then pay to receive a code that activates some "crippled" features, like the ability to print or to use advanced functions.

Both shareware and freeware are often accompanied by a license agreement that sets forth the terms and conditions of use of that product. Though shareware is commercial software, many shareware authors use electronic distribution as part of their distribution system. Loading shareware onto or downloading shareware from the Internet does not constitute piracy. However, shareware may be considered pirated if it is not registered and paid for before the expiration of the application's specified trial period.

While there is no money exchanged to obtain a copy of freeware and it can usually be downloaded without liability, freeware can still be considered to be pirated if it is used in a manner that violates an accompanying agreement. For example, if the freeware license contains a restriction on selling the freeware and someone includes the freeware on a compilation CD of freeware programs and sells the program, the freeware has been pirated because the license has been violated.

Unlike shareware or freeware, there are no copyright restrictions on a piece of public domain software. Therefore, public domain software will usually not be subject to a license agreement and the user of public domain software is generally free to use the software as they desire, with no restriction.

Internet Piracy

Internet piracy is the most rapidly expanding type of piracy and the most difficult form to combat. Internet piracy takes many forms:

- Auction site piracy;

- Bulletin board services & news group piracy;

- FTP [file transfer protocol] sites;

- Warez;

- Peer-to-peer;

- Cracks/serial numbers sites; and

- Internet relay chat.

Auction site piracy occurs when the seller burns software onto CD-ROMs, offers the software for sale in an online auction. The auctioneer will often data-mine the names and e-mails of losing bidders and contact those bidders in an attempt to sell additional copies. SIIA has a good working relationship with most major auction sites and is able to remove pirate auctions shortly after their being posted. . . .

FTP allows one to upload files and download files to a site. Software pirates who transfer programs to one another commonly use FTP sites because it is efficient for transferring large files and most FTP servers support some form of anonymous login. . . .

Peer-to-peer [P2P] technologies allow users to communicate in real-time and transfer files to each other. Because of the distributed and often anonymous nature of P2P sites, they are widely used for distribution of unauthorized software and content. P2P networks are also popular because they are basically "one stop shopping" where a user can find just about anything they are looking for—music, software, movies. Of all the forms of piracy discussed, P2P piracy is the most difficult to stop. . . .

Web sites, often called *warez sites*, allow the downloading of software—generally free of charge—from the Web.

> *"Nearly everything is subject to counter-*
> *feiting today—from medications to air-*
> *plane parts."*

Counterfeiting Consumer Goods Is Copyright Infringement

Laura Palotie and Alexandra Zendrian

In the following viewpoint, Laura Palotie and Alexandra Zen-
drian claim an array of consumer products—such as lighters,
designer handbags, and video games—are being counterfeited
and passed off as the geniune article, which infringes on copy-
rights. The manufacturing boom in China has dramatically in-
creased the sales of counterfeit goods, the authors insist, resulting
in mounting revenue losses and job layoffs. Palotie is a journalist
based in New York City. Zendrian is a business reporter for Inc
.com, the Web site for Inc., a monthly magazine for small busi-
nesses and entrepreneurs.

As you read, consider the following questions:

1. How has counterfeiting affected the lighter company
   Zippo and its employees, in Palotie and Zendrian's view?

Laura Palotie and Alexandra Zendrian, "Attack of the $35 Gucci Handbag," Inc.com,
April 28, 2008. Copyright © 2008 Mansueto Ventures LLC. All rights reserved. Repub-
lished with permission of Inc.com, conveyed through Copyright Clearance Center, Inc.

2. What is the magnitude of national and global economic losses due to counterfeiting, according to the authors?

3. Why do Palotie and Zendrian claim that fighting counterfeiters is an "exhaustive process"?

The Zippo lighter, a streamlined metal rectangle that opens and closes with a signature snap, has been a favorite among smokers for more than 75 years. But that simple, iconic design has also made it a favorite among counterfeiters.

"This is not rocket science," says Jeff Duke, Zippo's general counsel. "Anybody involved in light-metal manufacturing could gear up to make this product. Obviously we have sophisticated equipment, and we make it better and faster than anybody in the world, but there really isn't anything we can do to stop the counterfeiters from copying it."

Although all of Zippo's pocket lighters are produced at its headquarters in Bradford, Pa., anywhere between 5 and 50 percent of lighters bearing the Zippo name sold across the globe are fake, the company estimates. (Asia, Eastern Europe, and South America are counterfeit hotspots, according to Zippo.) [In 2006] such rip-off Zippos were cutting into the company's revenue by about 25 percent, and Zippo was forced to layoff 15 percent of its workforce—121 employees altogether.

Tracy Burgess had been assembling Zippo BLU butane lighters for about a year when she got the news. Work in the factory had been slowing down for some time and rumors were circulating about possible layoffs, but Burgess stayed positive. Zippo had kept its workers busy enough in hopes that business would pick up, she recalls.

"One day, they finally came and said they had to let us go," Burgess says. "It was embarrassing, because I cried like a baby. It was the first time I had been laid off. And even though it was a layoff, it felt like I was being fired. There's still that feeling that you've let down the company or you've done something personally wrong."

"Most of the people I worked with were new hires," Burgess adds. "It went from sadness to some anger. There was a sense of despair. We are a small town here, and 121 people in a town this size is a lot of people."

The company's story is not uncommon: Losses from counterfeiting and piracy lead to the loss of more than 750,000 American jobs, the U.S. Chamber of Commerce estimates.

Since the company began cracking down, with the help of investigators, police, and customs officials, Zippo's overall sales have since picked up about 10 percent, Duke says. But the problem is far from eliminated—about 10,000 finished lighters and hundreds of thousands of lighter components were seized at Chinese factories [in 2007] alone. In China, Zippo mainly relies on the work of one private investigation firm that tracks down illegal manufacturing sites and alerts local law enforcement. The actual raids are conducted by China's Administration of Industry and Commerce and the People's Security Bureau.

The rise in sales is reason to be optimistic, Duke says, especially taking into account widespread anti-smoking campaigns, which inevitably reduce the demand for lighters. As a result, most employees who lost their jobs in 2006, including Burgess, were given a chance to come back.

Common Counterfeit Targets

While luxury brands, such as Dolce & Gabbana and Louis Vuitton, are common counterfeit targets, Zippo is an example of everyday items that are increasingly subject to knockoff. Piracy, of course, is not a new concept, but the International AntiCounterfeiting Coalition, a Washington-based non-profit, estimates that the number of counterfeit products on the market has surged 10,000 percent over the past two decades. At least part of the growth stems from the manufacturing boom in China, where many counterfeit goods wind up being produced in the very same factories that make the real ones.

Counterfeit buyers, tempted by $25 Coach purses and $10 Dolce & Gabbana sunglasses may only see a bargain, but both the U.S. and global economies take a hit as a result. The U.S. Chamber of Commerce estimates that the U.S economy loses between $200 and $250 billion in annual sales due to counterfeiting, while the world economy is robbed of about $650 billion every year. A 2007 study by the Institute for Policy Innovation, Lewisville, Texas-based think tank, claims that copyright theft costs the U.S. economy $58 billion in lost output and $2.6 billion in lost tax revenue.

Nearly everything is subject to counterfeiting today—from medications to airplane parts. According to a report released [in 2007] by the Department of Homeland Security, the top three types of items seized on U.S ports of entry were footwear (the equivalent of $77 million in authentic goods), apparel ($27 million), and consumer electronics ($16 million). However, those statistics represent just goods that were seized, which is a small fraction of overall counterfeit activity.

Large companies with ubiquitous brand names naturally make the biggest targets. In 2007, video game giant Nintendo lost $975 million in revenue due to piracy alone, and seized nearly 2 million pieces of pirated software. Commercial success of the company's Wii and DS consoles has resulted in a demand for cheap alternatives, says Jodi Daugherty, Nintendo of America's senior director of anti-piracy. To prevent piracy, she says, game developers embed security measures into all software—code that makes it more difficult to copy games.

Pirated electronics can also present a significant safety risk, Daugherty points out. [In 2007] a seven-year-old British boy was electrocuted and killed when his parents unknowingly purchased a knockoff Nintendo Game Boy adaptor in Thailand.

Nintendo trains customs officials around the world to recognize knockoff Nintendo products, and has reached out to the U.S. trade representative [federal agency that negotiates

"Fake Potter books in China," cartoon by Paresh Nath, *The National Herald*, India. Copyright 2007 by Paresh Nath and CagleCartoons.com. All rights reserved.

trade agreements] to enact more aggressive anti-counterfeiting legislation. Countries such as Mexico, Brazil, and China are particularly challenging for Nintendo's market because their local counter-piracy laws have not effectively halted a rampant counterfeiting culture.

An Exhaustive Process

Fighting against counterfeiters is often an exhaustive process for companies, especially smaller ones short on resources and manpower. Once the counterfeited company has gathered proof that suspicious products are indeed fakes, it can approach the U.S. Immigration and Customs Enforcement and the U.S. Patent and Trademark Office. Brand-protection companies can help catch instances of online counterfeit sales, while private investigators can take counterfeits out of the market. Businesses are also increasingly turning to local authorities, like the economic crimes division of some local police forces.

Andrew Oberfeldt, a private investigator at New York-based Abacus Security, says that simply alerting authorities is not enough—companies need to train customs and security in identifying their products and hire investigators who can be a 24-hour contact for law enforcement.

"It's like drug smuggling," Oberfeldt says. "There's so much money and it's so multifaceted that if you aren't doing it on every level, you're not doing anything."

"My mantra is that customs offices and officers are your best friend," adds Barbara Cason, intellectual property director at Columbia Sportswear, a company that seized 250,000 counterfeit items in 2005. "Not only do they provide the opportunity to register your trademark, but they also have opportunities for brand owners to come and present their products and show what an authentic or a fake looks like."

With trendy labels, advertisements for counterfeits appear in countless junk mail inboxes as physical products are strewn over discount street vendor racks. When a brand gains momentum, companies are encouraged to take action sooner rather than later. If a counterfeiting industry has time to take off, it becomes that much more difficult to extinguish.

"If you have a leak in your roof and you let it grow over weeks and months, it becomes a lot bigger of a problem," says Frederick Felman, chief marketing officer of MarkMonitor, a San Francisco, Calif.-based brand-protection company. It's very similar in the counterfeiting world. If you don't treat something, other people start to pile on and start abusing and copying your brand. But if you take action, it makes the economics of it less interesting, so they move on to a brand that isn't defended."

Some companies are taking a more grassroots approach. Abercrombie & Fitch, Coach, and Estee Lauder, among others, have partnered with the International AntiCounterfeiting Coalition [IACC] to create a college outreach program, which provides case studies to marketing and public relations classes at schools like Harvard and New York University. Students get the opportunity and funding to practice crafting their own [public relations] campaigns—through blogs, Facebook, and fashion shows, and other efforts—while the IACC raises awareness and enlists supporters for its effort.

No matter how focused the efforts, however, links on the counterfeiting chain are difficult to break. Factory raids might cause an individual manufacturer to lose inventory and machinery, but those running the operations from a distance are tough to identify.

"We end up raiding manufacturers and have a very hard time figuring out who really is behind all of it," Zippo's Duke says. Although the number of fake lighters on the Chinese market has dropped about 10 percent [from 2006 to 2008], their quality seems to have picked up, he says.

"Without any question, we are still losing 15 percent" of total sales, he says. "That's a very big number."

Periodical Bibliography

Amy J. Benjamin and John LaBarre — "Donating Works to the Public Domain Isn't Always the Best Way to Provide the Public Access to Your Work," *Licensing Journal*, June–July 2006.

Janet L. Conley — "Copyright Suit Tests How Much Is Too Much," *Fulton County Daily Report*, April 18, 2008.

K. Matthew Dames — "Making a Case for Copyright Officers," *Intellectual Property*, July–August 2008.

Mary Jane Frisby — "Speed Trap on the Information Highway: Copyright Law," *Indiana Business Journal*, March 17, 2008.

Robert M. Goodman — "The Boundaries of Copyright," *Digital Video Magazine*, July 1, 2006.

Lev Grossman — "The Battle over Music Piracy," *Time*, May 24, 2007.

Brian Grow et al. — "Dangerous Fakes," *Business Week*, October 13, 2008.

Clark Hoyt — "Culling the Anonymous Sources," *New York Times*, June 8, 2008.

Ann Hulbert — "How Kaavya Got Packaged and Got into Trouble," *Slate*, April 27, 2006.

Aaron Krowne and Raymond Puzio — "The Fog of Copyleft," *First Monday*, July 3, 2006.

Managing Intellectual Property — "Copyright Minefield of Second-hand Software," December 2006.

Laura Possessky — "Can I Use It? First Amendment and Rights Clearances," *Maryland Bar Journal*, March–April 2007.

Dana Thomas — "The Fake Trade," *Harper's Bazaar*, January 2008.

CHAPTER 2

What Facilitates Copyright Infringement?

Chapter Preface

In cyberspace, "aXXo" is a modern-day Robin Hood. The anonymous teenager is the most popular movie uploader on BitTorrent, a peer-to-peer (P2P) network. According to file-sharing blog TorrentFreak, some of aXXo's in-demand "torrents" are downloaded between 500,000 and a million times a week. "If I see a great film I believe everyone has the right to be entertained by it," he supposedly declared in an online interview. Many file sharers prize aXXo's torrents because of their digital clarity, lack of viruses and other pesky malware, and lighting-fast turnaround (he uploads many movies ahead of their DVD release), earning him an abundance of notoriety on blog posts: "I dont know what I would do without him"; "Axxo uploads are the only ones I don't hesitate to download"; "I hope axxo goes to prison for life. Thats where you belong, for making such amazing dvd-quality rips."

However, that is precisely why the Motion Picture Association of America (MPAA) and numerous major studios want to see aXXo behind bars, or at least stopped for good. In November 2007, aXXo removed his torrents from the Pirate Bay, an online file-sharing index, over alleged MPAA intervention. Speculation has also emerged that the trade association is waiting for aXXo to turn 18 to prosecute him. Moreover, studios are clamping down on illegal file sharing, and aXXo's downloaders are more likely to be singled out for infringement. In March 2008, a college student posted on Torrent-Freak that using the notorious torrents resulted in a notice from the major movie studio NBC Universal and a meeting with university officials.

With gains in broadband speeds and improved compression technologies, critics uphold that P2P networks have become the greatest threat to the film, music, and content industries. In the following chapter, the authors examine how copyright infringement may be enabled.

> *"The rise of many P2P services ... and the dramatic decline in music and video sales have prompted the recording industry to take aggressive legal actions on a global scale to curtail unauthorized distribution of copyrighted materials."*

Peer-to-Peer Services Facilitate Copyright Infringement

Alan C. Chen

In the following viewpoint, Alan C. Chen contends that peer-to-peer (P2P) file-sharing technology facilitates the unauthorized distribution of copyrighted works on a global scale, sending music and video sales into a decline. In response, he says, the recording industry and its partners have filed—and won—numerous lawsuits against P2P services around the world for contributory and vicarious copyright infringement. Additionally, the author notes that the recording industry has identified, and filed lawsuits against, individuals engaging in unauthorized file-sharing, producing mixed public reaction and results. Alan C. Chen is a Los Angeles attorney specializing in media, entertainment, and technology.

Alan C. Chen, "Copy Locally, Share Globally: A Survey of P2P Litigation Around the World and the Effect on the Technology Behind Unauthorized File Sharing," *Intellectual Property & Technological Law Journal*, vol. 19, no. 9, September 2007, pp. 1–4. Copyright © 2007 Aspen Publishers, Inc. All rights reserved. Reproduced by permission.

As you read, consider the following questions:

1. How did the U.S. Supreme Court rule in the recording industry lawsuits against Grokster and Kazaa?

2. According to Chen, why did the Dutch court rule in favor of Kazaa in *Buma/Stemra v. Kazaa*?

3. In Chen's opinion, why is digital rights management (DRM) not a solution to illegal file-sharing?

The advent of peer-to-peer file-sharing technology (P2P) has made it easy for people to freely distribute, download, and copy audio and videos in digital format anywhere in the world. While the original concept behind P2P was to empower peers within a network of computers to share resources, the rise of many P2P services such as Napster and Grokster and the dramatic decline in music and video sales have prompted the recording industry to take aggressive legal actions on a global scale to curtail unauthorized distribution of copyrighted materials.

Traditionally, the recording industry only targets P2P services and Internet service providers (ISP) that make available the means for consumers to engage in unauthorized file-sharing. Since 2003, however, the recording industry began filing lawsuits against users of P2P services who are allegedly major uploaders of infringing content, adding to the recording industry's list of targets tens of thousands of consumers each year from all walks of life around the world. Ironically, those consumers are also the recording industry's target customers.

To appreciate the effect of litigations against P2P services and the technology behind it, following are brief summaries of the lawsuits against P2P services in the United States, Australia, Japan, Korea, Taiwan, and the Netherlands and a description of the impact of the lawsuits on technological developments and the future of P2P services.

Curtail P2P File-Sharing via Lawsuits Against P2P Services

In 1982, the recording industry sued Sony in the United States for manufacturing and distributing Betamax recorders, which allowed consumers to record television broadcasts. In that case, the court ruled that Sony's manufacture and distribution of the recorders were not infringing because the product and its technology had substantial non-infringing uses. Similarly, a UK court ruled in 1988 that the manufacturer of a cassette tape recorder is not liable for copyright infringement because the manufacturer did not "procure infringement" by advertising attractions of the machine to any purchaser who may decide to copy unlawfully.

At the turn of the century, with the rapid deployment of broadband for use in conjunction with personal computers all around the world, copying and sharing have taken on an entirely different scale and dimension. With the growing popularity of P2P services such as Napster, Grokster, and Kazaa, consumers could download and copy exact duplicates of protected works anywhere in the world without the traditional physical constraints. As a result, global sales of music and videos declined significantly, and the recording industry rallied its partners from all around the world to file lawsuits against P2P services.

United States: Napster, Grokster, Kazaa, and Lime Wire

In *A&M Records v. Napster*, The Ninth Circuit ruled in favor of the recording industry by finding Napster liable for both contributory and vicarious copyright infringement. The court based its ruling on Napster's use of a centralized indexing system for tracking files and managing connections between peers on its network. Because of the tracking capability, the court found that Napster also had the ability to control and filter files to prevent unauthorized file-sharing. Subsequently, new and evolving P2P services attempted to circumvent liability using the lessons learned from *Napster* by creating decentralized file-indexing solutions, as is the case with the popular P2P services Grokster, Kazaa, Aimster, Bit Torrent, and Lime Wire.

On June 13, 2002, a group of US recording industry heavyweights jointly filed a copyright infringement lawsuit against Grokster and Kazaa. On June 27, 2005, the US Supreme Court ruled in favor of the recording industry by finding that the P2P services were liable for infringing acts of their end users if they distributed "a device with the object of promoting its use to infringe copyright, as shown by clear expression or other affirmative steps taken to foster infringement" (the inducement theory).

Unlike the ruling in *Napster*, the Supreme Court shifted the analysis of liability away from the technical framework of the P2P network to the overall conduct of its creators or owners. Accordingly, P2P services are evaluated, in addition to its software design, by its overall business behavior such as its marketing, interaction with end users, efforts to curtail illicit file-sharing, and how revenue is generated.

After the *Grokster* ruling, many popular P2P services, including eDonkey, BearShare, WinMx, and Bit Torrent, announced their intentions to cooperate with the recording industry to stop illegal file-sharing. However, after changing their business model of distributing only licensed content, many services, including BearShare, Aimster (a.k.a. Madster), and Grouper, eventually closed shop entirely.

Most recently, the recording industry filed a lawsuit against Lime Wire for copyright infringement. Predictably, the recording industry asserted that Lime Wire should be held liable based on the inducement theory, as well as contributory and vicarious infringement. This will be the first case after *Grokster* for testing the resolve and reach of the inducement theory in the US courts. Additionally, this case may provide further opportunities for the court to explain the applicability of contributory and vicarious liability on a decentralized P2P network.

Australia: Kazaa

In Australia, the recording industry successfully sued Kazaa, in the matter of *Universal Music Australia v. Sharman License Holdings LTD*. In that case, the Australia federal court ruled in the recording industry's favor by finding that Sharman Networks [owner of Kazaa] had knowledge of and "authorized" the infringing uses of its software and had a direct financial interest in the infringing activities. The owners of Kazaa were ordered to pay US$115 million in damages. However, the federal court gave Kazaa the option to remain in operation subject to its adoption of a keyword filter technology to identify infringing content or, alternatively, limiting the search results to non-infringing works.

Japan: MMO

In Japan, the Recording Industry Association of Japan brought a lawsuit against Japan MMO, a P2P service, in the matter of *Nippon Columbia Co., Ltd. v. Yugen Kaisha Nippon MMO*. Unlike most other P2P services sued recently. Japan MMO used a centralized indexing system like Napster for tracking files. In ruling for the recording industry, the Tokyo District Court found that Japan MMO had played a central role in the infringing acts of the end users who were violating the copyright owners' exclusive right under the law. As a result of the lawsuit, Japan MMO was enjoined from offering its services and was found liable for copyright infringement. Japan MMO was ordered to pay US$350,000 in damages plus interest.

Korea: Soribada

Soribada, also known as the Korean Napster, was originally a P2P service with a centralized index of shared files. Eventually, Soribada evolved into a decentralized system that distributed both paid and free copyrighted works. In August 2005, the Seoul Central District Court ordered Soribada to be shut down following a series of lawsuits filed by the local recording industry. The court ruled that Soribada had aided and abetted copyright infringement based on the finding that Soribada had knowledge of infringing activities by its users, derived profits from such infringing activities, and failed to implement filters to limit infringing activities. In focusing on the conduct of the P2P service, the court disregarded the decentralized index structure of the software entirely.

Concurrently with the civil lawsuit, the two principals of Soribada were also charged with criminal aiding and abetting of copyright infringement. However, the criminal charges were eventually dismissed on the ground that the two operators did not break any copyright law by creating the Soribada software, even though end users may have.

Taiwan: Kuro

In the first criminal conviction involving P2P services, Kuro, the most popular subscription-based P2P service in Taiwan, and its three principals were convicted of criminal copyright infringement in September 2005. The Taipei Shilin District Court based its ruling on the finding that Kuro and its principals were fully aware of the illegal downloads on their services but continued to attract subscribers and earned fees through advertisements, which boasted the availability of its vast collection of unlicensed materials. In addition, the principals were each fined US$90,000 and sentenced to between four months to three years in confinement.

In a separate civil lawsuit between the local recording industry and Kuro, the parties reached settlement following the criminal conviction for US$9 million.

The Netherlands: Kazaa

In the only favorable case for P2P services around the globe, Kazaa received validation for its non-infringing uses in *Buma/Stemra v. Kazaa* in the Netherlands. In that case, a Dutch collecting society representing music writers and publishers sued Kazaa based on substantially the same factual underpinning as those in *Grokster* in the United States. The Dutch court of appeals found that, while Kazaa did provide the means for unauthorized publication and reproduction of copyrighted works, providing the means is not an act of publication or reproduction. The court's ruling cited Kazaa's many non-infringing uses and relied heavily on the finding that it is not possible for Kazaa to distinguish, on a technical level, which of the files shared through its network is infringing.

Sue the Consumer by the Thousands

Although lawsuits against P2P services have been fairly successful in courts throughout the world, the recording industry insists that unauthorized file-sharing using new and alternative P2P services continues to increase. To further stem the tide of unauthorized file-sharing, the recording companies around the world are coordinating their efforts to target users of the P2P services. Under the banner of raising public awareness about the illegality of unauthorized file-sharing, the recording industry began suing consumers directly and systematically all around the world. As of 2007, the recording industry has filed more than 36,000 lawsuits in 18 countries against individual end users of P2P services. Because of strict liability for copyright infringement and the individual lawsuits' nuisance value, nearly all cases have been settled without trial. According to the recording industry, the average settlement is US$3,000 per case.

The recording industry identifies individual consumers for lawsuits by sending undercover investigators to participate in P2P services to download unlicensed materials from other users within the same P2P network. Once the files are downloaded and verified as infringing, the uploader's information, including the Internet protocol (IP) address, is logged as evidence. Using the IP address, the recording industry will subpoena the account holder's identity and file suit.

The recording industry's aggressive enforcement of its copyright has been met with some criticism from consumers. Particularly, there was a flurry of negative publicity during the

The Internet and Copyright Infringement

The recent development of computer technology—most notably the Internet—has had a complex and profound effect on the dissemination of copyrighted works, by the copyright holder and by infringers alike. Both the supply of, and the demand for, copyrighted works have escalated dramatically because of the Internet's success as a communications medium, the large number of people worldwide who use it, and the ease with which materials may be made available for copying. Media products produced today, including software and music, are often in a digital format, which permits fast, cheap, and easy production of copies (legitimate or infringing) identical in quality to the original. The digital nature of today's media products also makes them much easier to distribute in large scale over the Internet. . . .

In Internet-based copyright cases, experience has shown that certain issues arise regularly: (1) large scale infringement without profit motive; (2) disclaimers; (3) unusual proof issues for quantity, loss, and identity; and (4) sympathetic defendants including juveniles. Moreover, Internet-based copyright cases often involve complex, emerging technologies, which raise unique legal and technical issues that require additional background, including: (1) novel means of infringement; (2) facilitation; (3) audio compression technology such as MP3; and (4) file sharing technologies.

David Goldstone and Michael O'Leary,
"Novel Criminal Copyright Infringement Issues Related
to the Internet," U.S. Department of Justice, April 26, 2005.

first few waves of such lawsuits because of mistakes in identifying the correct parties. Since the majority of P2P users are not the heads of households whose names appear on the bills linking them to the unique IPs that identify the end users, substantial investigation is often required to identify the correct party to the lawsuit. For homes with unsecured wireless networks, the P2P user may even be a neighbor and not a member of the household. In one such case, the RIAA [Recording Industry Association of America] erroneously named a 12-year-old girl living in a public housing project in New York City as a defendant. In another, a grandmother living in Massachusetts who only used a Macintosh computer was accused of using Windows-only Kazaa to download music illegally.

Despite mixed public reaction in those lawsuits, the recording industry appears to be a firm believer in the effectiveness of its tactics targeting consumers. The recording industry cites consumers' fear of lawsuits as a significant factor in lowering the amount of unauthorized P2P activity. The recording industry believes that unauthorized P2P activity has been contained since the lawsuits targeting consumers began. The recording industry reports that, in 2003, the number of infringing music files on the Internet dropped from its peak of 1.1 billion to about 885 million in 2006, while broadband penetration in households rose by 139 percent during the same period. However, critics of the recording industry's tactics offer conflicting data and research showing that P2P activity, when measured by the number of P2P users, more than doubled between 2003 and 2006. Moreover, critics argue that many users have now moved beyond P2P networks for file-sharing, leaving those alternative file-sharing activities unaccounted for by most empirical metrics.

Regardless of whether unauthorized P2P activity has been effectively contained, the lawsuits targeting consumers are apparently successful in raising the level of awareness that unauthorized downloading of copyrighted works is illegal and can have serious consequences. However, it remains to be seen whether increased public awareness will directly translate into a decrease in unauthorized file-sharing activities.

The Technology Behind File-Sharing Within the Current P2P Framework

Because recent court decisions tend to focus less on technological aspects of P2P services and more on inducement, the technology behind P2P has not advanced as dramatically as in the aftermath of the *Napster* decision. In general, the changes evolve around making the P2P services more secure and covert to minimize the risk of exposure to the services and end users alike.

To maintain a greater level of security and covertness, many P2P services began to mask the identities of their end users, the content of the files being shared, or both. To mask the identities of end users, some P2P services simply forego logging of end users' access on its servers, including end users' IP and the index of their shared content. For masking the shared content, some P2P services encrypt all shared data to guard against casual snooping. However, encryption is not completely secure since the encryption keys used by many P2P services are also readily accessible to the recording industry's investigators.

P2P services can also channel data through intermediate Internet connections that obfuscate the download source as well as origin of file requests. For instance, some P2P services and end users use pseudonymous servers or anonymous proxy servers to reroute connections so that the peers within the networking group cannot identify each other.

Going beyond P2P services' internal framework, end users can also conceal their identities [in various other ways on the network]. . . .

New Technology to Prevent Unauthorized Copying and Distribution via P2P Networks

Although most courts appear to favor finding liability against P2P services for their role in enabling, contributing, and inducing copyright infringement, file-sharing proponents continue to develop new technology to challenge the very limits of law. Accordingly, the recording industry must also rely on aggressive pursuit of innovation to stay ahead of the technical challenges.

Digital Rights Management

Digital Rights Management (DRM) refers to the technology used by copyright owners to control access and usage of digital data. The technology typically involves the use of an encryption algorithm to scramble data so that it cannot be played without proper authorization or software. For instance, music purchased via the popular iTunes music download service contains a DRM technology called FairPlay. FairPlay-protected music can be played only on iTunes and iPods, subject to further limitations on the number of times that the music can be duplicated for personal use. [1]

While many people consider DRM to be an effective tool in preventing unauthorized copying, it is not the solution to unauthorized P2P activities. First, paid music downloading services such as iTunes are not P2P services technically. Second, because DRMs are proprietary, their interoperability is limited. The lack of interoperability prevents the licensee from enjoying the downloads on third-party software and hardware platforms. Finally, DRM is susceptible to hacks and leaks, which may require constant maintenance and development to prevent the technology from falling into irrelevance in the long run.

---

1. On January 6, 2009, Apple and several major record labels reached an agreement to remove FairPlay restrictions.

Hash-Based Filtering

Lime Wire, one of the early adapters of the decentralized index system for P2P services, developed a filter to block files based on certain metadata (hash) unique to each work. The unique hash can be used to identify copyright works but requires cooperation from copyright owners to provide hashes to Lime Wire. However, Lime Wire's use of hash-based filtering has met with significant resistance because of many copyright owners' reluctance to adopt the technology. The reluctance may be based on the fear of violating the proprietary rights for a similar hash-based filtering system owned by competing business interests, including the recording industry.

Digital Fingerprinting

The recording industry has also been advocating for the use of digital fingerprinting technology to identify copyrighted material being shared via P2P networks. The technology creates a unique identifier based on the wave form or algorithms of a music or video file. The identifier makes it possible to monitor, track, manage, and filter the copyright works by intercepting packets of data being transmitted between peers on the Internet. However, this technology can be overcome by the use of encryption to protect data being sent between peers. The encryption would make the music being transferred unrecognizable to ordinary investigation tools.

The Future of File-Sharing: Beyond P2P

Because of rapid evolutions in computer technology, there is no one technology that has an absolute and clear advantage in securing or overcoming unauthorized file-sharing activities. Players on either side of the P2P file-sharing debate can and will continue to create countermeasures against each other, as the recording industry's repeated triumph in courtrooms around the world has not translated into a full abatement of unauthorized copying activities on P2P networks. Even if all the present P2P services are eventually stamped out of existence because of lawsuits, the premises giving rise to the popularity for unauthorized file-sharing remain: As long as technology continues to provide relatively easy means to share files without the usual cost associated with their purchases, many consumers will continue to embrace the less costly option. To that end, alternate and effective means of file-sharing without the P2P network scheme, such as instant messaging and digital stream ripping technology, are becoming increasingly popular. Such other alternatives may eventually overtake P2P services as the technology of choice for unauthorized file-sharing.

"Although the early use of P2P networks was for digital piracy, P2P networks are increasingly being used for legitimate content distribution, including music, video and software."

Peer-to-Peer Services Can Be Legitimized

Knowledge@Wharton

In the following viewpoint, the author contends that peer-to-peer (P2P) sites are regrouping and forming legitimate services that allow customers to share copyrighted music and video files while creating revenues for artists and the recording industry. For instance, the author claims that—in contrast to iTunes's more rigid model—P2P start-ups are offering flexible pricing for songs; the author also points out that to attract customers and encourage authorized file-sharing, others are paying referral fees to users to share in-demand or scarce music and video files. Knowledge@Wharton *is the online business publication of the Wharton School at the University of Pennsylvania.*

Knowledge@Wharton, "File-Sharing Networks Return with Legitimate Ways to Share Music—and Make Money," August 8, 2008. All materials copyright of the Wharton School of the University of Pennsylvania. Reproduced by permission.

As you read, consider the following questions:

1. How does a legitimate P2P service work, according to the author?

2. According to *Knowledge@Wharton*, why would a P2P service pay a referral fee that is higher than a track's price?

3. How does the file-sharing service We7 create revenue, as explained by the author?

After the U.S. Supreme Court declared in 2005 that Internet file-sharing sites Grokster and StreamCast had illegally aided their customers' efforts to share pirated copies of copyrighted music and video files, many commentators predicted the demise of businesses that depended on online file-sharing.

But the technology that Napster, the pioneer of music file-sharing, Grokster and StreamCast unleashed has returned, supported by a business plan that respects copyright laws. Three years after the high court's ruling, several start-ups say they have found ways to make peer-to-peer (often called P2P) file-sharing legal and perhaps profitable.

"Although the early use of P2P networks was for digital piracy, P2P networks are increasingly being used for legitimate content distribution, including music, video and software," writes Kartik Hosanagar, a Wharton professor of operations and information management, in a recent paper on P2P business models. "For example, Grooveshark, rVibe, We7 and iMesh are firms that use P2P networks to distribute music to users. The music is licensed from the music labels, the files are distributed from users' machines and the P2P firms provide software and billing. A number of technologies have also emerged to prevent piracy in P2P networks. As a result, distribution of digital products through P2P networks is likely to become more prevalent."

Still, Hosanagar says that these new commercial outfits need to tweak their business plans. He predicts that they will make more money if they are savvier about pricing content and about paying their customers to share it. In "Dynamic Referrals in Peer-to-Peer Media Distribution," Hosanagar and two co-authors at the University of Washington, Yong Tan and Peng Han, create a mathematical model of the ebb and flow of supply and demand on a peer-to-peer network. Their model suggests that file-sharing firms should often pay high fees to users who provide content to other users—sometimes higher than the retail price of the file itself—and that they should vary these referral fees and their prices according to the demand for particular files. (The three scholars have also recently completed a related paper on the topic titled, "Diffusion Models for Peer-to-Peer (P2P) Content Distribution: On the Impact of Decentralized, Constrained Supply.")

How P2P Networks Operate

To appreciate their arguments, it helps to understand how peer-to-peer file-sharing works.

Each computer in a peer-to-peer network acts as both a store and a customer. Users of these networks can provide content by making the files on their computers available to other users of the network. In return, they can use the network to reach into other customers' computers and copy the files that have been made available. Participants in a peer-to-peer network can share any kind of content, though music has proved most popular. The P2P networks provide software that enables their customers to organize their content, search the network and swap files with each other. These firms often charge a fee for each file acquired though the network, and use that revenue to pay royalties to content creators and referral fees to users who share their files.

An obstacle to the growth of these networks, the paper's authors write, is that many customers are eager to copy files but reticent to make their own files available to others, a practice called free riding. The free riders may have files that other users would like to have, but can't find. Vibe and Grooveshark try to induce free riders to share files by paying referral fees for making the files available to other customers. But Hosanagar says that they may not be paying enough. "rVibe pays 5 cents for a 99-cent track. Grooveshark has recently changed its policy, but I think it was originally 10 cents a song. Our conclusion is that you want to offer really high payments early on and that payments shouldn't be fixed. We found in many cases that the [referral] payment could be higher than the price. For example, you might initially pay $1.50 for a 99-cent file."

Why would a company pay more for a product than the eventual sale price? Is that not a recipe for bankruptcy? Not at all, Hosanagar says. It's a logical response to the law of supply and demand. "The initial high payment brings in a lot of distributors, and it gets them to share files when there's scarcity." As a result, he says, the firm ensures that its customers can get the files they want and don't shop elsewhere or resort to illegal file-sharing. By encouraging early distribution, the arrangement also feeds the buzz that any media company seeks: as more and more people hear a song or see a video, they may recommend it to friends who then may buy it, too. Those users, in turn, distribute the file, scarcity abates, and the firm can gradually reduce the referral fee.

Let Demand Determine Price

Retail prices for content on a peer-to-peer network should work similarly, Hosanagar says. That is, they should be flexible and reflect demand. Firms would then have two pricing options. If they want to create buzz, they may initially set a low price for files to encourage people to buy them. Or they may decide to price based on scarcity, charging more early on to capture maximum revenue from the zealots who'll snap up anything new from a favorite artist. Later, once that hardcore

A Huge Opportunity for Games Publishers

While the music industry merrily sues its customers for illegal file sharing, there's another part of the entertainment industry trying a radically different approach. Games publishers are actually working with peer-to-peer networks to sell legitimate versions alongside all the illicit copies. And early signs suggest it's working.

Games publishers know that pirated copies of their games are on the ever-growing number of P2P networks like Kazaa, Overnet and Grokster. But what they've also realised is that these same networks can be used to distribute legitimate copies that can be virus protected and will get technical support. . . .

"200m people regularly play, download or look for games content online. That's more than the number who buy at retail," says Gabe Zichermann, [vice president] of strategy and communications of Trymedia, an anti-piracy software firm. Trymedia provides around 300 legitimate games . . . on P2P networks and has seen 20m downloads in the past 18 months alone. Those numbers of people and downloads are a huge opportunity for games publishers.

Dominic Dudley, "Guerrilla Gameplay,"
New Media Age, *September 25, 2003.*

demand has been sated, they could charge less. "The optimal strategy seems to be to price the product low at first and pay the majority of the amount [collected] to the P2P distributor," Hosanagar says. "So initially your profits are lowest. Over time, you increase your price and reduce your referral payments." On the Internet, firms can easily implement flexible prices. "In the past, it was difficult to do customized pricing," notes Hosanagar. "The music industry has generally been one that was slow to adapt."

Anyone who has bought a song from the popular iTunes store might wonder why peer-to-peer firms don't forego all of these hassles and organize themselves like Apple, with tightly policed central servers. Apple controls the content on its website and sets the terms of use, including its famed fixed price of 99 cents for any song.[1] Its customers can then count on songs always being available. "It's extremely expensive to distribute media centrally," Hosanagar notes. "An Apple has the capital and expertise to manage that, but not everyone does." In contrast, P2P "allows a firm to efficiently distribute media at a relatively low cost," Hosanagar and his co-authors note. "Further, the distribution infrastructure automatically scales as new consumers join the network."

What's more, organizing a company as an enabler of peer-to-peer sharing potentially provides a wider menu of offerings for customers. "Apple is going to find it impractical to negotiate deals with a lot of independent, unknown artists, while with a Grooveshark or rVibe, the independent artist signs up for the service, creates an account and uploads his songs," says Hosanagar. That allows the artist's fans, no matter how small a group they are, to download songs and pay whatever price the artist and Grooveshark agree to (with Grooveshark taking a small percentage of each sale).

Likewise, that obscure musician will have a tough time arranging a distribution deal with iTunes. "Apple isn't going to want to negotiate contracts with a bunch of unknowns," Hosanagar points out.

The most ardent advocates of peer-to-peer networking argue that it will eventually displace Apple because consumers

1. On January 6, 2009, Apple announced it had reached an agreement with major music labels and was switching to a multi- tiered pricing structure.

will tire of Apple's inflexible pricing, and content providers will rebel against its stranglehold on online distribution.

"Personally, I don't see the P2P model displacing iTunes," Hosanagar says. "But I do think it's here to stay. I recollect a statement that I read in early 2000 where somebody said P2P was a solution in search of a problem. That's moot now," with many people around the world sharing files on legal peer-to-peer networks.

Still, the question remains: Can sharing become a booming business like iTunes? Certainly many consumers want to swap files online, but it's not as clear that they're willing to pay to do so. The brief history of file-sharing is littered with failed ventures.

In the Beginning

For practical purposes, Napster, the brainchild of a Northeastern University freshman, created the niche. The service allowed anyone to swap—or in the opinion of the major music labels, steal—music files online. If you wanted a song by the White Stripes and someone on the network shared it, you could download and play it on your PC. Napster kept, on a central server, an index of all the music available on its network, which made searching easy. Music labels sued, arguing that Napster was abetting the pirating of copyrighted music files. A federal court agreed and Napster was eventually liquidated.

When Grokster and StreamCast entered the market, they provided file-sharing software but didn't create central indexes. Their software allowed users to search each other's computers, seeking files that they wanted. When the major labels sued them, they argued that they couldn't control what people did with their software and, without central indexes, didn't even know. The U.S. Supreme Court didn't buy their arguments and ruled that they, too, had abetted theft.

But file-sharing lived on. Solid estimates of the extent of illegal file sharing are scarce, but some range as high as one billion songs a year. rVibe and Grooveshark are trying to persuade at least some of these folks to purchase downloads by combining appeals to guilt and greed. Grooveshark's website stresses that musicians go hungry if people don't pay for their music, and of course it pays those referral fees.

Rock musician Peter Gabriel has endorsed another approach. He's an investor in a peer-to-peer file-sharing firm called We7. Its customers can download free songs with short ads at the beginning. "The revenue generated from these advertisements goes to artists, labels and other rights owners," We7 explains on its website. "You get music for free, and the artist gets fairly paid." The ad disappears after four weeks. Or customers can elect to purchase a file outright and skip the ad. Users can also share files.

Which of these models will triumph? Hosanagar isn't sure.

"I can think of three or four outcomes we might see. There might be free content that's used to stimulate demand for the other things, like concerts and T-shirts. There might be free ad-supported content. Or there might be a model where you buy the songs, but it will not be the rigid pricing model that we see today. Or lastly, it might be a model where payment is on a per-play basis rather than a per-purchase basis."

> *"Viral video represents the use without charge of another's intellectual property."*

Viral Video Often Constitutes Copyright Infringement

Scott D. Marrs and John W. Lynd

In the following viewpoint, the authors maintain that many viral videos found on sites like YouTube violate copyright laws. According to Marrs and Lynd, copyright holders do not grant clearance or receive royalties for the use of their footage or work, negating the free publicity they may create. Although pursuing legal action against every instance of infringement and revenue loss due to viral videos is not feasible, Marrs and Lynd recommend that copyright holders work in conjunction with video-sharing sites to end unauthorized distribution and use and assert their intellectual property rights. Scott D. Marrs and John W. Lynd are attorneys who specialize in intellectual property litigation.

As you read, consider the following questions:

1. In Marrs' and Lynd's view, what are the economic harms of viral videos to copyright owners?

Scott D. Marrs and John W. Lynd, "Viral Videos Publicize—But Infringe," *National Law Journal*, May 8, 2008. Copyright © 2008 ALM Properties, Inc. All rights reserved. Further duplication is prohibited. Reprinted with permission.

2. Why do Marrs and Lynd argue that "mash-up" videos constitute copyright infringement?

3. What tips do the authors provide to copyright holders when faced with infringing activities?

W hat is "viral video?"

When a video clip spreads quickly across the Web, it is described as "going viral." You have likely already encountered viral video, those sometimes interesting, amusing or even entertaining pieces of video attached to email messages like: "Check this out, it's hilarious!" But where did that video footage come from, who owns it and what are the economic and legal implications of this activity?

These video clips usually originate on viral video Web sites (free video-sharing sites), where users of the site can view, upload, download and share clips with others, spreading the clip far and wide, literally worldwide, without cost, and often without the permission of the owner of the copyrighted video footage.

Viral video is proliferating on the Web in two ways: first, through the straightforward posting and sharing of video clips without modification, and, second, through the visual remixing of copies of clips. The remixed video is often referred to as a "mash-up," where different video materials are juxtaposed together, or where numerous clips from one film or television show are borrowed and compiled with altered dialogue or theme music, for comic effect. These mash-ups are then posted on viral video sites and shared.

What does viral video mean to television networks, movie studios and other owners of copyrighted video material? The viral use of copyrighted material without the owner's permission ultimately has a detrimental effect, since the work is not being viewed by the public in its intended form or location. The copyright owner derives economic benefit when the video is viewed in its intended location, namely, in movie theaters, via rented or purchased DVD/video recordings, on its television channel or on its own Web site (or a site licensed to stream that content). After all, that is why "works of authorship" are given protection under the law. Viral video represents the use without charge of another's intellectual property.

Copyright owners are beginning to realize the full import of what was once only a pesky problem. NBC Universal Inc. recently led an investigation of free video-sharing sites where its copyrighted material was being used without license. The site, YouTube.com, was acting as a conduit for the free sharing of a 2 1/2-minute spoof rap (entitled "Lazy Sunday: Chronicles of Narnia") from NBC's *Saturday Night Live*. NBC served You-Tube with a "cease and desist" notice demanding it remove this footage and approximately 500 other clips from its site or face legal proceedings for copyright infringement. YouTube immediately complied. . . .

It has been reported that NBC then engaged in a "search-and-destroy" mission to shut down other free video-sharing sites where its copyrighted material was being used without permission. Although it has refused to identify the sites it has investigated, NBC has indicated that it uncovered more than 3,000 videos being shared without permission, including entire episodes of its television show *Will and Grace*, the feature-length movie *Brokeback Mountain* and hours of NBC's coverage of the recent Winter Olympics.

Copyright Issues

Is viral video copyright infringement, and if so, what remedies are available to copyright owners? This article assumes that the video clips being used by video-sharing sites are protected by the Copyright Act. Although Congress established a voluntary system of registration, it created incentives for copyright owners to register their copyrights. The most significant benefit to registering copyrights under the act is the right to enforce a copyright in federal court. Infringement suits are the mechanism through which other important incentives and remedies created by the act operate.

For example, when actual damages are difficult to ascertain or a creative work has seemingly little extrinsic value, statutory damages are available. Statutory damages can be between $750 and $30,000 for each infringing work. Damages can therefore add up quickly when, as with viral video, there are sites sharing thousands of clips of copyrighted material without the owners' permission. If the court finds that the infringement was willful, it may increase the award of statutory damages to $150,000 per infringed work. Equally important in the litigation context, a certificate of registration is prima facie [sufficient] evidence of copyright validity. For copyright owners hesitant to engage in the long and expensive process of litigation, costs and attorney fees for prevailing parties may be recovered. Finally, and perhaps most important, a registrant can obtain an injunction against an infringer.

NBC succeeded in stopping the activities of YouTube without resorting to litigation. However, if an owner of copyrighted video material does file suit against an alleged infringer for viral video activities, it will have to convince a court that this kind of video sharing constitutes copyright infringement. There are two things a plaintiff must prove to establish a prima facie case of copyright infringement: that it owns the allegedly infringed material (i.e., it is the copyright owner), and that the alleged infringer violated at least one of the exclusive rights granted to the plaintiff. Those rights include the exclusive right to reproduce the copyrighted work, to prepare derivative works based upon the copyrighted work, to distribute copies of the work and to display the work publicly.

The U.S. Supreme Court held recently [2005] in *MGM Studios Inc. v. Grokster Ltd.* that a distributed file-sharing system commits copyright infringement when its principal object is the dissemination of copyrighted material. The foundation of this holding was a belief that people who post or download music files without the copyright owners' permission are primary infringers. This activity is directly analogous to the activities of viral video sites. Therefore, the courts are likely to conclude that the posting of video clips to these sites and their subsequent sharing represents copyright infringement, and are activities for which the remedies mentioned above are available. A caveat to this conclusion, however, is that although the posting and sharing of unaltered video clips without the copyright holder's permission represents infringement, matters are not so clear-cut with regard to video remixes or mash-ups.

Mash-ups and Fair Use

A recent example of a video remix/mash-up is a clip entitled "Must Love Jaws." This remix includes excerpts from the 1975 classic movie *Jaws*, and is recast as a feel-good *Free Willy*-type aquatic adventure for comic effect. . . . This example illustrates the fact that video remixes or mash-ups are derived from the pre-existing work or works used to make the remix or mash-up. A derivative work is defined as a work based upon one or more pre-existing works and that includes works that recast, transform or adapt that pre-existing work to create something new. Video remixes fall within this category. The right to prepare derivative works belongs exclusively to the copyright owner. Therefore, the use of video clips in this way, without the copyright owner's permission, is arguably, on its face, also copyright infringement.

If charged with copyright infringement, mash-up artists will likely assert the statutory defense of fair use. When confronted with this defense, the Copyright Act provides that a court must take into account the purpose and character of the use, including whether it is of a commercial nature or is for nonprofit educational purposes; the nature of the copyrighted

YouTube's "Safe Harbour" Provisions

Whether YouTube is infringing copyright or not, simply by hosting infringing content on its website, is arguable. . . .

For example, the US Digital Millennium Copyright Act 1998 (DMCA) contains "safe harbour" provisions, which protect ISPs [Internet service providers] and website operators against copyright infringement. To be within the DMCA safe harbour provisions, YouTube and similar video hosting websites must have, among other things, implemented a notification and takedown system which allows copyright owners to notify them of any infringement and quickly remove alleged infringing content. YouTube has implemented such a system and other measures to fit within the "safe harbour" provisions, but with so much content being uploaded every day, it is inevitably hard to police.

Simpson Grierson, "Will Copyright Infringement Kill the Video (Sharing) Star?" December 2006. www.simpsongrierson.com.

work; the amount and substantiality of the portion used in relation to the copyrighted work as a whole; and the effect of the use upon the potential market for, or value of, the copyrighted work. These factors and their application to any fair use determination depend heavily upon the individual facts and circumstances of each case.

In *Campbell v. Acuff-Rose Music Inc.*, the Supreme Court held that commercial parody may be considered "fair use." The [Supreme] court held that the 6th U.S. Circuit Court of Appeals [which held that the parody was not fair use] did not give sufficient consideration to the nature of the parody involved in that case (2 Live Crew's rap parody of Roy Orbison's song "Oh, Pretty Woman") and had placed too much weight on the song's commercial character and the amount of content borrowed from the original. The court carried out an exhaustive analysis of the fair-use factors in reaching its decision to reverse the 6th Circuit's ruling.

Although concurring, Justice Anthony Kennedy had some words of warning to those who would interpret the court's ruling as blanket permission for parodists to infringe the copyrights of others: "[P]arody may qualify as fair use only if it draws upon the original [work] to make humorous or ironic commentary about that same composition. . . . As future courts apply our fair use analysis, they must take care to ensure that not just any commercial take-off is rationalized post hoc as a parody."

In light of the holding in *Campbell*, some analysts have assumed that video remixes/mash-ups currently proliferating on the Web (such as "Must Love Jaws") are now free game and shielded from assertions of copyright infringement by the fair use defense. However, this is not a certainty, and much will depend on the nature of the activity involved, and whether the remixers want to run the risk of being hauled into federal court to face allegations of copyright infringement and then have to rely upon the fair use defense, which will always be subject to the discretion of the fact finder, and thus prone to uncertainty.

Tips for Copyright Owners

If faced with infringing activities, copyright owners should be aware that a cause of action for infringement accrues when one has knowledge of a violation or is chargeable with such knowledge. In a case of continuing infringement, however, an action may be brought for all acts that accrued within the three years preceding the filing of the suit.

Copyright owners should also be aware that their rights to pursue injunctive relief and/or a claim for actual or statutory damages may be barred by the doctrine of copyright estoppel. This doctrine applies when the alleged infringer can show that the copyright owner knew the facts of the infringement; the copyright owner intended its conduct to be acted upon or acted in a manner giving the alleged infringer a right to believe it was so intended (in other words, the copyright owner led the alleged infringer to believe that it didn't mind the infringing activity); the alleged infringer is ignorant of the true facts; and the alleged infringer relies on the copyright owner's conduct to his detriment.

Further, a copyright owner can be estopped not only by words and actions, but also by silence and inaction. The message to copyright owners is: Act as soon as these types of activity come to light, and utilize the remedies available under the Copyright Act if matters cannot be resolved by other means. Of course, viral video by its nature proliferates and propagates easily, and takes on a life of its own, making it a daunting task for anyone, even the largest network or studio, to investigate and take action against every instance of infringement.

How may copyright owners address viral video without pursuing infringement action? Viral video may amount to free publicity, but it ultimately results in no immediate or tangible economic benefit to the copyright owner, which is, after all, the primary benefit to copyright protection. However, it is apparent from the number of people viewing and sharing video clips and video remixes that there is a demand. It has been reported that NBC's investigation revealed that some of its videos had been downloaded more than 5 million times. The question then is, given the popularity of viral video, despite its legal implications and the remedies available to copyright owners under the law, should television networks and movie studios take a different approach (other than litigation) to this phenomenon?

One suggested solution is for television networks and other video copyright owners to partner with the most popular sites. It has been reported that a few established media companies have formed partnerships with YouTube:

"Independent recording label Matador Records is [promoting] the band Pretty Girls Make Graves by allowing viewers to submit music videos for its upcoming single. Cable network MTV2 has provided clips from upcoming programming including 'The Andy Milonakis Show' that links back to the MTV2 Web site. Even advertisers are on board, as Nike has seeded the site with video clips promoting its footwear. [In May 2006], Disney's Dimension Films entrusted YouTube with the trailer for its upcoming film 'Scary Movie 4,' which promptly garnered 200,000 streams in its first 15 hours on the site."

Another proposed solution is the establishment of an organization modeled on the existing performing rights societies which include the American Society of Composers, Authors and Publishers, Broadcast Music Inc. and the Society of European Stage Authors and Composers. Thousands, perhaps even millions, of times each day, musical works are performed publicly on the radio and on the Internet. Every performance represents a possible source of revenue for the copyright owner. However, given the huge numbers of broadcasts involved, this presents an insurmountable management problem for individual copyright owners.

In order to address this problem, composers and publishers of musical works have formed performing rights societies to control access to their works, license and police their use, and distribute fees/royalties collected to participating members by pooling their rights. Video copyright owners may consider forming an analogous organization to control the use of video footage (television shows, movies, etc.). This could provide an economical and centralized process for the legal use of copyrighted video footage with consistent results and appropriate remuneration to copyright owners.

In conclusion, viral video often constitutes copyright infringement, and remedies are available to copyright owners to address that activity. Although the posting and sharing of video clips is without doubt free publicity, it is also the free use of the owner's intellectual property, resulting in a loss of revenue to the owner. The very nature of this activity, its proliferation and the all but impossible task of policing every instance of infringement demands pragmatic solutions to its future management.

> "Video makers have the right to use as much of the original work as they need to in order to put it under some kind of scrutiny. Comment and critique are at the very core of the fair use doctrine as a safeguard for freedom of expression."

Many Viral Videos Use Copyrighted Materials Legally

Patricia Aufderheide and Peter Jaszi

In the following viewpoint, Patricia Aufderheide and Peter Jaszi discuss uses and principles that allow online video creators to incorporate copyrighted works within the doctrine of fair use. According to Aufderheide and Jaszi, "commenting on or critiquing" of copyrighted material "are at the very core of the fair use doctrine as a safeguard for freedom of expression." Nonetheless, posting a copyrighted work on a Web site to trigger discussion or in personal video pastiches or collages may not always be supported by fair use, the authors contend, especially if the purpose of the posting is not clear. Patricia Aufderheide is a film and media arts professor at American University in Washington, D.C.,

Patricia Aufderheide and Peter Jaszi, "Code of Best Practices in Fair Use for Online Video," July 7, 2008. www.centerforsocialmedia.org. Reproduced by permission.

and director of its Center for Social Media. Peter Jaszi is a law professor at American University's Washington College of Law.

As you read, consider the following questions:

1. Why were the provisions of fair use intentionally made nonspecific, according to the authors?
2. Why is positive commentary defensible under fair use, in Aufderheide's and Jaszi's opinion?
3. According to Auferderheide and Jaszi, can a fair use argument be used for archiving vulnerable materials or revealing copyrighted materials? Why or Why not?

... Video is increasingly becoming a central part of our everyday landscape of communication, and it is becoming more visible as people share it on digital platforms. People make and share videos to tell stories about their personal lives, remixing home videos with popular music and images. Video remix has become a core component of political discourse, as the video "George Bush Don't Like Black People" and the "Yes We Can" parodies demonstrated. Both amateur and professional editors are creating new forms of viral popular culture, as the "Dramatic Chipmunk" meme and the "Brokeback to the Future" mashup illustrate. The circulation of these videos is an emerging part of the business landscape, as the sale of YouTube to Google demonstrated.

More and more, video creation and sharing depend on the ability to use and circulate existing copyrighted work. Until now, that fact has been almost irrelevant in business and law, because broad distribution of nonprofessional video was relatively rare. Often people circulated their work within a small group of family and friends. But digital platforms make work far more public than it has ever been, and cultural habits and business models are developing. As practices spread and financial stakes are raised, the legal status of inserting copyrighted work into new work will become important for everyone.

It is important for video makers, online service providers, and content providers to understand the legal rights of makers of new culture, as policies and practices evolve. Only then will efforts to fight copyright "piracy" in the online environment be able to make necessary space for lawful, value-added uses.

Mashups, remixes, subs, and online parodies are new and refreshing online phenomena, but they partake of an ancient tradition: the recycling of old culture to make new. In spite of our romantic cliches about the anguished lone creator, the entire history of cultural production from Aeschylus through Shakespeare to *Clueless* has shown that all creators stand, as Isaac Newton (and so many others) put it, "on the shoulders of giants."

In fact, the cultural value of copying is so well established that it is written into the social bargain at the heart of copyright law. The bargain is this: we as a society give limited property rights to creators, to reward them for producing culture; at the same time, we give other creators the chance to use that same copyrighted material without permission or payment, in some circumstances. Without the second half of the bargain, we could all lose important new cultural work just because one person is arbitrary or greedy.

Copyright law has several features that permit quotations from copyrighted works without permission or payment, under certain conditions. Fair use is the most important of these features. It has been an important part of copyright law for more than 150 years. Where it applies, fair use is a right, not a mere privilege. In fact, as the Supreme Court has pointed out, fair use keeps copyright from violating the First Amendment. As copyright protects more works for longer periods than ever before, it makes new creation harder. As a result, fair use is more important today than ever before.

Copyright law does not exactly specify how to apply fair use, and that is to creators' advantage. Creative needs and practices differ with the field, with technology, and with time. Rather than following a specific formula, lawyers and judges decide whether an unlicensed use of copyrighted material is "fair" according to a "rule of reason." This means taking all the facts and circumstances into account to decide if an unlicensed use of copyright material generates social or cultural benefits that are greater than the costs it imposes on the copyright owner.

Fair use is flexible; it is not uncertain or unreliable. In fact, for any particular field of critical or creative activity, lawyers and judges consider expectations and practice in assessing what is "fair" within the field. In weighing the balance at the heart of fair use analysis, judges refer to four types of considerations mentioned in the law: the nature of the use, the nature of the work used, the extent of the use and its economic effect. This still leaves much room for interpretation, especially since the law is clear that these are not the only necessary considerations. In reviewing the history of fair use litigation, we find that judges return again and again to two key questions:

- Did the unlicensed use "transform" the material taken from the copyrighted work by using it for a different purpose than that of the original, or did it just repeat the work for the same intent and value as the original?

- Was the material taken appropriate in kind and amount, considering the nature of the copyrighted work and of the use?

Both questions touch on, among other things, the question of whether the use will cause excessive economic harm to the copyright owner.

If the answers to these two questions are "yes," a court is likely to find a use fair. Because that is true, such a use is unlikely to be challenged in the first place.

Another consideration underlies and influences the way in which these questions are analyzed: whether the user acted reasonably and in good faith, in light of general practice in his or her particular field. Online video makers' ability to rely on fair use will be enhanced by the Code of Best Practices in Fair Use that follows. This code of best practices serves as evidence of commonly held understandings—some drawn from the experience of other creative communities (including documentary filmmakers) and supported by legal precedents, and all grounded in current practice of online video. Thus, the code helps to demonstrate the reasonableness of uses that fall within its principles.

Video makers can take heart from other creator groups' reliance on fair use. For instance, historians regularly quote both other historians' writings and textual sources; filmmakers and visual artists reinterpret and critique existing work; scholars illustrate cultural commentary with textual, visual, and musical examples. Equally important is the example of commercial news media. Fair use is healthy and vigorous in daily broadcast television news, where references to popular films, classic TV programs, archival images, and popular songs are constant and routinely unlicensed.

Unlike many traditional creator groups, nonprofessional and personal video makers often create and circulate their videos outside the marketplace. Such works, especially if they are circulated within a delimited network, do enjoy certain copyright advantages. Not only are they less likely to attract the attention of rights holders, but if noticed they are more likely to receive special consideration under the fair use doctrine. That said, our goal here is to define the widely accepted contours of fair use that apply with equal force across a range of commercial and noncommercial activities, without regard to how video maker communities' markets may evolve. Thus, the principles articulated below are rooted squarely in the concept of "transformativeness."

In fact, a transformative purpose often underlies an individual creator's investment of substantial time and creative energy in producing a mashup, a personal video, or other new work. Images and sounds can be building blocks for new meaning, just as quotations of written texts can be. Emerging cultural expression deserves recognition for transformative value as much as more established expression.

Best Practices

This code of practices is organized, for ease of understanding, around common situations that come up for online video makers. These situations do not, of course, exhaust the possible applications of fair use to tomorrow's media-making techniques.

But first, one general comment: Inevitably, considerations of good faith come into play in fair use analysis. One way to show good faith is to provide credit or attribution, where possible, to the owners of the material being used.

One: Commenting On or Critiquing of Copyrighted Material

Description: Video makers often take as their raw material an example of popular culture, which they comment on in some way. They may add unlikely subtitles. They may create a fan tribute (positive commentary) or ridicule a cultural object (negative commentary). They may comment or criticize indirectly (by way of parody, for example), as well as directly. They may solicit critique by others, who provide the commentary or add to it.

Principle: Video makers have the right to use as much of the original work as they need to in order to put it under some kind of scrutiny. Comment and critique are at the very core of the fair use doctrine as a safeguard for freedom of expression. So long as the maker analyzes, comments on, or responds to the work itself, the means may vary. Commentary may be explicit (as might be achieved, for example, by the addition of narration) or implicit (accomplished by means of recasting or recontextualizing the original). In the case of negative commentary, the fact that the critique itself may do economic damage to the market for the quoted work (as a negative review or a scathing piece of ridicule might) is irrelevant.

Limitation: The use should not be so extensive or pervasive that it ceases to function as critique and becomes, instead, a way of satisfying the audience's taste for the thing (or the kind of thing) that is being quoted. In other words, the new use should not become a market substitute for the work (or other works like it).

Two: Using Copyrighted Material for Illustration or Example

Description: Sometimes video makers quote copyrighted material (for instance, music, video, photographs, animation, text) not in order to comment upon it, but because it aptly illustrates an argument or a point. For example, clips from Hollywood films might be used to demonstrate changing American attitudes toward race; a succession of photos of the same celebrity may represent the stages in the star's career; a news clip of a politician speaking may reinforce an assertion.

Principle: This sort of quotation generally should be considered fair use and is widely recognized as such in other creative communities. For instance, writers in print media do not hesitate to use illustrative quotations of both words and images. The possibility that the quotes might entertain and engage an audience as well as illustrate a video maker's argument takes nothing away from the fair use claim. Works of popular culture typically have illustrative power precisely because they are popular. This kind of use is fair when it is important to the larger purpose of the work but also subordinate to it. It is fair when video makers are not presenting the quoted material for its original purpose but to harness it for a new one. This kind of use is, thus, creating new value.

Limitations: To the extent possible and appropriate, illustrative quotations should be drawn from a range of different sources; and each quotation (however many may be employed to create an overall pattern of illustrations) should be no longer than is necessary to achieve the intended effect. Properly attributing material, whether in the body of the text, in credits, or in associated material will often reduce the likelihood of complaints or legal action and may bolster a maker's fair use claim.

Three: Capturing Copyrighted Material Incidentally or Accidentally

Description: Video makers often record copyrighted sounds and images when they are recording sequences in everyday settings. For instance, they may be filming a wedding dance where copyrighted music is playing, capturing the sight of a child learning to walk with a favorite tune playing in the background, or recording their own thoughts in a bedroom with copyrighted posters on the walls. Such copyrighted material is an audio-visual found object. In order to eliminate this incidentally or accidentally captured material, makers would have to avoid, alter, or falsify reality.

Principle: Fair use protects the creative choices of video makers who seek their material in real life. Where a sound or image has been captured incidentally and without pre-arrangement, as part of an unstaged scene, it is permissible to use it, to a reasonable extent, as part of the final version of the video. Otherwise, one of the fundamental purposes of copyright—to encourage new creativity—would be betrayed.

Limitation: In order to take advantage of fair use in this context, the video maker should be sure that the particular media content played or displayed was not requested or directed; that the material is integral to the scene or its action;

that the use is not so extensive that it calls attention to itself as the primary focus of interest; and that where possible, the material used is properly attributed.

Four: Reproducing, Reposting, or Quoting in Order to Memorialize, Preserve, or Rescue an Experience, an Event, or a Cultural Phenomenon

Description: Repurposed copyrighted material is central to this kind of video. For instance, someone may record their favorite performance or document their own presence at a rock concert. Someone may post a controversial or notorious moment from broadcast television or a public event (a Stephen Colbert speech, a presidential address, a celebrity blooper). Someone may reproduce portions of a work that has been taken out of circulation, unjustly in their opinion. Gamers may record their performances.

Principle: Video makers are using new technology to accomplish culturally positive functions that are widely accepted—or even celebrated—in the analog information environment. In other media and platforms, creators regularly recollect, describe, catalog, and preserve cultural expression for public memory. Written memoirs for instance are valued for the specificity and accuracy of their recollections; collectors of ephemeral material are valued for creating archives for future users. Such memorializing transforms the original in various ways—perhaps by putting the original work in a different context, perhaps by putting it in juxtaposition with other such works, perhaps by preserving it. This use also does not impair the legitimate market for the original work.

Limitation: Fair use reaches its limits when the entertainment content is reproduced in amounts that are disproportionate to purposes of documentation, or in the case of archiving, when the material is readily available from authorized sources.

Five: Copying, Reposting, and Recirculating a Work or Part of a Work for Purposes of Launching a Discussion

Description: Online video contributors often copy and post a work or part of it because they love or hate it, or find it exemplary of something they love or hate, or see it as the center of an existing debate. They want to share that work or portion of a work because they have a connection to it and want to spur a discussion about it based on that connection. These works can be, among other things, cultural (Worst Music Video Ever!, a controversial comedian's performance), political (a campaign appearance or ad), social or educational (a public service announcement, a presentation on a school's drug policy).

Principle: Such uses are at the heart of freedom of expression and demonstrate the importance of fair use to maintain this freedom. When content that originally was offered to entertain or inform or instruct is offered up with the distinct purpose of launching an online conversation, its use has been transformed. When protected works are selectively repurposed in this way, a fundamental goal of the copyright system—to promote the republican ideal of robust social discourse—is served.

Limitations: The purpose of the copying and posting needs to be clear; the viewer needs to know that the intent of the poster is to spur discussion. The mere fact that a site permits comments is not enough to indicate intent. The poster might title a work appropriately so that it encourages comment, or provide context or a spur to discussion with an initial comment on a site, or seek out a site that encourages commentary.

Six: Quoting in Order to Recombine Elements to Make a New Work That Depends for Its Meaning on (Often Unlikely) Relationships Between the Elements

Description: Video makers often create new works entirely out of existing ones, just as in the past artists have made collages and pastiches. Sometimes there is a critical purpose, sometimes a celebratory one, sometimes a humorous or other motive, in which new makers may easily see their uses as fair under category one. Sometimes, however, juxtaposition creates new meaning in other ways. Mashups (the combining of different materials to compose a new work), remixes (the re-editing of an existing work), and music videos all use this technique of recombining existing material. Other makers achieve similar effects by adding their own new expression (subtitles, images, dialog, sound effects or animation, for example) to existing works.

Principle: This kind of activity is covered by fair use to the extent that the reuse of copyrighted works creates new meaning by juxtaposition. Combining the speeches by two politicians and a love song, for example, as in "Bush Blair Endless Love," changes the meaning of all three pieces of copyrighted material. Combining the image of an innocent prairie dog and three ominous chords from a movie soundtrack, as in "Dramatic Chipmunk," creates an ironic third meaning out of the original materials. The recombinant new work has a cultural identity of its own and addresses an audience different from those for which its components were intended.

Limitations: If a work is merely reused without significant change of context or meaning, then its reuse goes beyond the limits of fair use. Similarly, where the juxtaposition is a pretext to exploit the popularity or appeal of the copyrighted work employed, or where the amount of material used is excessive, fair use should not apply. For example, fair use will not apply when a copyrighted song is used in its entirety as a sound track for a newly created video simply because the music evokes a desired mood rather than to change its meaning; when someone sings or dances to recorded popular music without comment, thus using it for its original purpose; or when newlyweds decorate or embellish a wedding video with favorite songs simply because they like those songs or think they express the emotion of the moment.

Conclusion

These principles don't exhaust the possibilities of fair use for online video. They merely address the most common situations today. Inevitably, online video makers will find themselves in situations that are hybrids of those described above or will develop new practices. Then, they can be guided by the same basic values of fairness, proportionality, and reasonableness that inform this code of practices. As community practices develop and become more public, the norms that emerge from these practices will themselves provide additional information on what is fair use. . . .

> *"Ultimately though, if there were no customers, there would be no knockoff business."*

The Growing Market of Counterfeit Goods Facilitates Copyright Infringement

Tim Phillips

In the following viewpoint, Tim Phillips contends that counterfeiting consumer goods has grown into a thriving and sophisticated global enterprise that flouts intellectual property laws. While counterfeiters have diversified and now knockoff every manufactured good imaginable, Phillips claims that efforts of the government, law enforcement, and brand owners to combat this problem have not expanded. He argues that as fakes become commonplace, customers will continue having difficulty viewing counterfeiting as a problem, or understanding the value of intellectual property, which will keep counterfeiters in business. Tim Phillips is the author of Knockoff: The Deadly Trade in Counterfeit Goods.

Tim Phillips, "Counterfeiting Becomes a REALLY Big Business," *Manufacturing & Technology News*, vol. 13, no. 3, February 6, 2006. Copyright © Publishers & Producers. All rights reserved. Reproduced by permission.

As you read, consider the following questions:

1. According to Phillips, what kind of environments become centers of counterfeiting?

2. How does Phillips support his claim that brand owners are not fighting counterfeiting effectively?

3. What actions does the author recommend to fight counterfeiting?

"A newly released congressional report calls for 'direct and forceful action' by the federal government to halt the distribution of bogus goods," according to an article in [trade magazine] *Discount Store News.* "Product counterfeiting is a rapidly growing problem which seriously threatens the health and safety of consumers."

The report, detailing the early involvement of organized crime in the counterfeiting business, was published in May 1984, and like many well-intentioned statements produced by government agencies world-wide on the subject of counterfeiting, it attracted brief press interest before disappearing from view. If the threat wasn't serious enough to mandate action [in 1984], is it any worse now?

"Knockoff Incorporated"

Since 1984, one thing about counterfeiting has certainly changed: the scale and danger of the crime. It is approximately 100 times larger now than it was then. The organized crime gangs that were fingered in the government's 1984 report have expanded their business into a sophisticated global enterprise. Yet the response from government, law enforcement and even the affected brands looks much the same. "Knockoff Incorporated" is now twice the size of Wal-Mart. Knockoffs account for 7 percent of world trade. Arguably it's the business success story of the modern era.

Counterfeiters have diversified. In researching my book, *Knockoff The Deadly Trade In Counterfeit Goods,* I encountered everything from counterfeit tea bags, filled with the floor sweepings from a tea factory, to entire fake gasoline stations. There is little today that can't be counterfeited for profit. We know about designer purses and watches, but that's only 4 percent of the business today, and gives a fake impression of the fake business.

Counterfeiters now have also globalized successfully, free from tariffs, quotas and working visas; united by the desire for a quick buck. Since China's accession to the WTO [World Trade Organization] in 2001, its manufacturing centers have opened up to the West. Try Chaosan if you are shopping for fake electronics and CDs; try Wenzhou City for bogus auto spares; in Yuxiao County, it's counterfeit cigarettes; and Jintan City has factories where you can get great deals on knockoff pesticides. Today, two-thirds of the counterfeits in the world come from mainland China, but centers for counterfeiting exist wherever there is low-cost manufacturing and lax law enforcement.

In Israel, Arabs and Jews co-operate to distribute counterfeit products. In Paraguay, investigators discovered a CD pressing plant run by Hong Kong Chinese. And in 2005 in Lagos, Nigeria, 17 Chinese entrepreneurs were discovered running an illegal CD pressing plant with 11 lines.

The counterfeiting trade exploded in 2001 due to the terrorist attacks. Tightened banking regulations meant it was harder for criminals to store cash, so reinvesting it in a cash-generative business like counterfeiting makes sense. The War on Terror changed priorities in law enforcement, diverting attention away from 'harmless' crimes like counterfeiting and focusing Customs inspectors' attention on other threats.

It's tough for consumers to decide there's a problem when they see the same counterfeits openly on sale in the flea markets, Internet sites and local stores where they live, week after week. Far from being intolerable—as the CEOs [chief executive officers] of the entertainment, clothing, drugs, auto and software business claim—a certain level of counterfeiting is clearly tolerated in the developed world. Consumers might forgive brand owners and governments when those counterfeits are purses, but they will not be so indulgent when they hear about the counterfeit cancer treatments, brake pads made from sawdust and bogus aircraft parts that are part of the business too.

Who tolerates this? We all do.

The military is often accused of fighting the previous war with its technology and tactics. It seems that those in charge of fighting the knockoff business have the same characteristic. No one can criticize those in the anti-counterfeiting business for lack of effort, but could the resources be used more productively?

First, many brand owners are still locked into the fallacy that their counterfeiting problem is their business alone. For example, for reasons not hard to understand, the auto business does not even try to measure the scale of counterfeiting in spare parts, or to estimate their effect on road safety. In many industries, information that may be useful to police and customs is rarely shared with them. There is no obligation and little incentive to inform customers of dangerous counterfeit products, and companies routinely work in isolation to enforce only against counterfeiters of their brand. If the counterfeiters switch brands, the problem has gone away—but it has actually just mutated. Recent history tells us that they will return. This is a long-term failure dressed up as a short-term success.

The Reality of the Problem

Law enforcement needs to accept the reality of the problem. One intellectual property lawyer told me that he was told by law enforcement that unless there was a dead body involved, "don't even pick up the phone." Law enforcement agencies are

A Chief Counterfeit Hub

New York City is one of the world's chief counterfeit hubs. In addition to being a major tourist and retail destination, the city's ports handle 13.4 percent of U.S. container traffic, providing ample opportunities for illegal shipping. For example, [in December 2007], the *New York Times* reported that federal officials seized over $200 million in smuggled goods at the Port Newark-Elizabeth Marine Terminal in New Jersey, including counterfeit Nike Air Jordan sneakers listed as "refrigerated noodles" on the ship's manifests.

Aubrey Fox,
"The High Price of Counterfeit Goods,"
Gotham Gazette, *March 31, 2008.*

overwhelmed by counterfeiting problems, but this is no excuse for a lack of coordinated and forceful action.

In the United States, the best example of this is New York's Office of Midtown Enforcement [now the Mayor's Office of Special Enforcement, which addresses various dangerous city conditions], where a group of brand owners cooperate with the police in high-profile raids on Manhattan warehouses known to contain counterfeit goods. The raids are deliberate shows of strength. The brand owners, many of whom are competitors in daily life, stand together against a common enemy.

Too often we're fighting a sophisticated global crime business with patchy local resources. Much of law enforcement against counterfeiting is regional or at best national; it needs the intelligence that global corporations can provide to work effectively.

Ultimately though, if there were no customers, there would be no knockoff business. If counterfeits become commonplace then we educate a generation of consumers that intellectual property has little value—at precisely the moment the developed world, with its high cost of manufacturing, is coming to rely on it as the engine of development. Some industries sue customers who pirate their product: The Business Software Alliance [BSA] is trying to educate its way out of the problem, experimenting with teaching the concept of intellectual property to eight year olds in elementary schools in Virginia. "We conducted research in 2004 asking 1,000 eight to 18 year olds about piracy," says Debbi Mayster at the BSA. "We found that they generally understood what piracy was. But they still do it."

It's time to stop pretending this problem can be fixed by calls to action, trade delegations and piecemeal private enforcement. Zero tolerance of counterfeiters through coordinated action between brand owners and law enforcement, married to the education of the next generation of consumers in the value of IP [intellectual property] will be time consuming and expensive—but it's not something that can be left to the federal government, or another [25] years may pass. Manufacturing industries and consumers are already paying the price of counterfeiting, and that price is getting steeper every day.

Periodical Bibliography

Stephanie C. Ardito   "Social Networking and Video Web Sites: MySpace and YouTube Meet the Copyright Cops," *Searcher*, May 2007.

Associated Press   "U.S. Firms Fighting the Flood of Fakes," July 7, 2006.

Kate Betts et al.   "The Purse-Party Blues," *Time*, August 2, 2004.

Michael Fricklas   "Our Case Against YouTube," *Washington Post*, March 24, 2007.

Wojciech Gryc and Jesse Helmer   "A Copyright Call to Arms," *Globe and Mail*, November 12, 2008.

Andy Guess   "Looking at Students and P2P—With Data," *Inside Higher Ed*, October 31, 2008.

Jon Healey   "Looking for Napster 2.0," *Los Angeles Times*, October 15, 2007.

Jeff Howe   "The Shadow Internet," *Wired*, January 2005.

Jonathan V. Last   "Google and Its Enemies," *Weekly Standard*, December 10, 2007.

Samuel Lewis   "Sampling or Stealing?" *Miami Daily Business Review*, November 21, 2006.

Jonathan Parkyn   "Get Your Fair Share," *Computeractive*, February 21, 2008.

Doris Tourmakine   "More Lowdown on Downloading: Illegal Capture of Movies Finds Common Acceptance," *Film Journal International*, June 2008.

Daniel B. Wood   "The YouTube World Opens an Untamed Frontier for Copyright Law," *Christian Science Monitor*, December 18, 2006.

OPPOSING VIEWPOINTS® SERIES

CHAPTER 3

What Are the Effects of Copyright Infringement?

Chapter Preface

According to the U.S. Patent and Trademark Office, the intellectual property of the United States is worth over $5 trillion. It accounts for more than half of the country's exports and drives 40 percent of its economic growth, claims the U.S. Chamber of Commerce. And the Federal Bureau of Investigation reports that counterfeiting and piracy costs the American economy between $200 and $250 billion in sales each year, resulting in the loss of 750,000 jobs, a number provided by U.S. Customs and Border Protection.

Advocates for stronger intellectual property laws frequently cite these data. For instance, Vermont senator Patrick Leahy refers to them in a July 2008 press release, and James P. Hoffa, general president of the International Brotherhood of Teamsters union, did so in 2007 testimony before the U.S. House of Representatives Subcommittee on Courts, the Internet, and Intellectual Property: "The total impact of these crimes is very real. Hundreds of billions of dollars per year in lost revenue and the resulting lost taxes, and millions of quality jobs."

Yet, skeptics are critical of the validity of such estimations. Julian Sanchez, Washington, D.C., editor of technology news site Ars Technica, argues, "These statistics are brandished like a talisman each time Congress is asked to step up enforcement to protect the ever-beleaguered U.S. content industry." He disputes the claim of 750,000 jobs lost, alleging that the figure is more than twenty years old, originally given by former secretary of commerce Malcolm Baldridge, who approximated job losses from counterfeiting to be "anywhere from 130,000 to 750,000." Furthermore, Sanchez insists that projected $200–$250 billion in losses may not calculate in the real world. "When someone torrents a $12 album that they would have otherwise purchased, the record industry loses $12, to be sure," he says. "But that doesn't mean that $12 has magically vanished from the economy. On the contrary: someone has gotten the value of the album and still has $12 to spend somewhere else."

Indeed, 750,000 jobs and $200–250 billion are alarming figures. They are intended to convey the harms of intellectual property theft, counterfeiting, and piracy in numbers that speak to working Americans—not just to economists and scholars. In the following chapter, the authors offer divergent views on economic and societal impacts of copyright infringement.

> "In sum, motion picture piracy affects not only the movie studios, but all the various businesses that supply the industry or buy from the industry, and the people who work in those businesses."

Copyright Infringement of Movies Hurts the Economy

Stephen E. Siwek

In the following viewpoint, Stephen E. Siwek argues that copyright infringement of major motion pictures has a cascade effect that harms the entire economy. He cites industry studies estimating that movie piracy costs Americans thousands of jobs and billions annually in earnings across a wide range of industries, and results in large tax revenue losses. To maintain the health of the U.S. economy and its global competitiveness, the author claims it is imperative that the government and policymakers work in concert to combat copyright infringement in the film industry. Stephen E. Siwek is a financial and cost-analysis consultant.

Stephen E. Siwek, "The True Cost of Motion Picture Piracy to the U.S. Economy," Institute for Policy Innovation: Policy Report 186, September, 2006, pp. 1–4. Copyright © 2006 Institute for Policy Innovation. Reproduced by permission.

As you read, consider the following questions:

1. According to Siwek, how does the movie industry's $6.1 billion loss in 2005 to piracy compare to the U.S. economy as a whole?

2. Why do pirates target major motion pictures, in the author's opinion?

3. How does Siwek demonstrate his claim that the U.S. economy is an "interlocking system"?

It is well-known that rampant piracy and counterfeiting of desirable products such as movies, recorded music, software, pharmaceuticals, and name-brand and designer consumer goods harm the bottom lines of the companies that produce these products. Because of the innovative and creative nature of our economy, U.S. companies are particularly vulnerable.

Companies work diligently to protect their products, employing civil enforcement, utilizing technology, and forming industry coalitions—as companies have in the U.S. through the United States Chamber of Commerce's Coalition Against Counterfeiting and Piracy (CACP)—to increase understanding of the scope of the problem and drive greater government-wide efforts to address this threat. Ultimately, however, given the global nature of the problem and its criminal character, government must play a crucial role in combating piracy and counterfeiting, and insisting on the enforcement of intellectual property rights as part of agreements with our trading partners.

Unfortunately, there has been little reliable economic information available to U.S. policymakers to assist them in balancing the importance of enforcing intellectual property [IP] rights against other priorities. To begin to address that problem, I published [in 2005] *Engines of Growth: Economic Contributions of the U.S. Intellectual Property Industries*, which examined the contributions to the U.S. economy of the "IP industries"—industries that rely most heavily on copyright or patent protection to generate revenue, employ and compensate workers, and contribute to growth. The study found, among other things, that these IP industries are the most important growth drivers in the U.S. economy, contributing nearly 40% of the growth achieved by all U.S. private industry and nearly 60% of the growth of U.S. exportable products. It also found that the IP industries are responsible for one-fifth of the total U.S. private industry's contribution to GDP [gross domestic product] and two-fifths of the contribution of U.S. exportable products and services to GDP.

But if the IP industries are worth protecting because of their contributions to the U.S. economy, policymakers still need sound information on the impact of piracy and counterfeiting on the U.S. economy to enable them to gauge the appropriate level of resources to deploy against the problem. To be sure, many industries cite statistics on piracy or counterfeiting losses specific to them, and some overall estimates of losses due to piracy and counterfeiting periodically surface in the media. But there is noticeably little data that reliably estimates the *total economic impact piracy and counterfeiting have on the U.S. economy*—including the impact on tax revenue, job creation, and economic output.

This study is a first step in this direction. It concentrates solely on movie piracy, taking as its starting point a recent comprehensive analysis that found that the major U.S. movie companies lost $6.1 billion in 2005 to piracy. Using methodology developed and maintained by the U.S. government, this study finds that the movie companies' $6.1 billion loss translates into total lost output among all industries of $20.5 billion annually. It also finds that lost earnings for all U.S. workers amounts to $5.5 billion annually, and 141,030 jobs that would otherwise have been created are lost. In addition, as a result of piracy, governments at the federal, state, and local levels are deprived of $837 million in tax revenues each year.

In the coming months, we will conduct additional analyses on other industries affected by counterfeiting and piracy, using similar methods to estimate the effects of piracy and counterfeiting in those industries on the U.S. economy. When the series of studies is completed, policymakers will have a much clearer picture of the true cost of piracy and counterfeiting to the U.S. economy.

This study, focused solely on the effects of piracy from one industry, suggests that the economic toll taken by copyright piracy and counterfeiting as a whole is enormous, and harms not only the owners of the intellectual property but all U.S. consumers and taxpayers. As policymakers seek to maintain the health and vitality of the U.S. economy and preserve our global competitiveness, the importance of recognizing the real costs of piracy and counterfeiting cannot be overstated.

Measuring the Harm Caused by Motion Picture Piracy

Because popular motion pictures are expensive to produce but cost almost nothing to illegally reproduce, they are a favorite target for pirates. Within days of their theatrical release—and in rare cases even before—most movies are available through DVDs sold on the street or by downloading illegally over the Internet.

In order to provide an accurate and detailed assessment of the film industry's worldwide losses due to piracy, in 2004 the Motion Picture Association of America (MPAA) commissioned a study by LEK Consulting, Inc. This study, based on extensive consumer surveys, determined what revenues the movie companies would have earned if pirated products had not been available. The result is the most comprehensive look at film piracy to date, capturing losses due to both Internet and hard goods piracy, the cost of piracy to domestic and worldwide industries, and the profile of the typical pirate in various market. . . .

A Fragile Fiscal Base

It is important to understand that the film industry rests upon a fragile fiscal base. Each film is a massive upfront investment with absolutely no guarantee of return. The average film costs over $100 million to make and market. Only one in ten films recoups this investment through its theatrical release. Six in ten films never break even. To recoup the considerable investment required to make and market a movie, the film industry relies on foreign distribution and ancillary markets (home video/DVD, pay per view, premium cable, basic cable, free TV, etc.) to make a profit or break even. It is these ancillary markets, especially home video and foreign distribution—economic engines that are essential to this industry—that are most vulnerable to the corrosive effects of film piracy.

Dan Glickman, "Testimony of The Honorable Dan Glickman Before the Subcommittee on 21st Century Competitiveness, Committee on Education and the Workforce," September 26, 2006.

The LEK study determined that the losses sustained from piracy to U.S. MPAA member companies in 2005 amounted to approximately $6.076 billion. But that figure reflects only the direct losses to the major motion picture studios themselves, and does not shed light on the overall effect of motion picture piracy on the U.S. economy.

Our Interlocking Economy

In order to understand how piracy in one segment of the economy can affect other industries, we must remember that the economy is an "interlocking" system. Changes in supply or demand in one industry can and do affect supply and demand in other industries.

For example, assume that personal watercraft, like Jet-Skis®, suddenly become very popular and shortages develop. In this situation, the price of personal watercraft will rise and so will the profits of the manufacturers. However, in order to continue to earn these higher profits, the manufacturers will have to make more personal watercraft. In the process, they will buy more waterproof seats from seat manufacturers.

Of course, it doesn't stop there. In order to produce more seats, the seat manufacturers will have to buy more plastic and more padding. And the plastic and padding manufacturers will have to buy more of the particular materials that they need.

The cascade does not end with the suppliers to personal watercraft manufacturers, but continues downstream as well. The retail sellers of personal watercraft who buy from the manufacturers will also be able to earn more money by raising prices or increasing volume. In their wake, specialty stores that customize personal watercraft or sell parts also stand to benefit.

These kinds of interactions among industries are captured in input-output tables. Input-output tables measure the inter-relationships that exist among different industries. With this information, one can then estimate what impact a specific change in one industry will have on other industries.

What is true for personal watercraft is equally true for motion pictures. If the revenue generated by making motion pictures increases (in this case, not by higher demand but by a decrease in piracy), movie companies will make more movies, invest in higher quality, broader distribution or more marketing, or some combination of these activities in order to capture more profits.

As more movies are made, or more is invested in making, marketing and distributing movies, the people and companies that supply movies will make more money. These include, for example, ad agencies, who sell more copy to newspapers and television promoting the films, and the newspapers and television stations that attract the increased revenue.

The benefits flow downstream as well. Video retailers, for example, will sell and rent more titles. Movie theaters will sell more tickets and more popcorn. Corn growers earn more profits, and can buy more farm equipment. And so on.

Put in economic terms, as motion picture output increases, so too would the output (sales of products and services) produced by these industries that supply motion pictures. As the output of these suppliers increases, so too would the output of other industries that supply the suppliers.

In sum, motion picture piracy affects not only the movie studios, but all the various businesses that supply the industry or buy from the industry, and the people who work in those businesses. Thus, the impact of movie piracy extends well beyond movie stars, all the way to the teenager selling popcorn and candy at the theater, the company that markets the candy, the farmer that grows the corn, and the workers that pick the farmer's crop.

> "*[Unauthorized] downloads may ex-plain a 30 percent reduction in the probability of buying music.*"

File-Sharing Copyrighted Music Hurts Music Sales

Alejandro Zentner

In the following viewpoint, Alejandro Zentner argues that file-sharing copyrighted music has resulted in a significant decrease in music purchases. The dramatic and continuing drop of global CD sales coincides with the creation of peer-to-peer (P2P) networks such as Napster and Kazaa, Zentner says, along with the spread of broadband Internet services. While acknowledging that recording industry lawsuits have decreased the size and popularity of P2P networks in recent years, Zentner believes that music sales continue to decline and online music piracy still surpasses licensed file-sharing and online music services. The author is an assistant professor in finance and managerial economics at the School of Management at University of Texas at Dallas.

As you read, consider the following questions:

1. How did the Recording Industry Association of America shut down Napster, according to the author's account?

Alejandro Zentner, "Measuring the Effect of File Sharing on Music Purchases," *Journal of Law and Economics*, vol. XLIX, April 2006, pp. 63–66, 68–71, 87–88. Copyright © 2006 University of Chicago Press. All rights reserved. Reproduced by permission.

2. How does the author contrast dial-up music downloading to broadband?

3. Why are music stores shrinking as a source of music
sales, in the author's view?

The global music industry was quite successful during the
1990s. According to the International Federation of the
Phonographic Industry (IFPI), album sales grew from US$24.1
billion in 1990 to US$39.4 billion in 1996 and remained at a
high level until 1999. Those days are over, and the industry is
now struggling. Global music sales have been falling. . . . Global sales (units) of CDs—the most popular format—fell in
2001 for the first time since its introduction in 1983.

This downturn coincides with the proliferation of online
music file sharing. In June 1999, Napster was created, making
the work of many artists available for free. Its popularity was
immediate. According to Mediametrix, a company that provides Internet rankings and measurement, Napster was the
fastest software adoption in history. Given its impact, the Recording Industry Association of America (RIAA) soon filed a
motion against Napster in the U.S. District Court of San Francisco for "engaging in or enabling, or facilitating others in
copying, downloading, uploading, transmitting, or distributing plaintiffs' copyrighted musical compositions and sound
recordings, protected by either federal or state law, without
express permission of the rights owner." Napster was shut
down in February 2001. However, many peer-to-peer alternatives for sharing music over the Internet remain available. In
2003, Kazaa claimed to be the most downloaded application,
with more than 230 million users worldwide. According to the
Yahoo Buzz Index, an index that measures Internet searches
using the Yahoo search engine, "Kazaa" was the number one
searched term on the Internet in 2003.

An Important Online Presence

File sharing has an important online presence. In May 2002, IFPI estimated that there were 3 million simultaneous global users and 500 million files available for copying at any given time. In 2002, NetPD, a company that provides protection services to copyright owners whose material is being pirated through the Internet, reported that 3.6 billion files were downloaded monthly, of which around 60–70 percent were music files. The most popular albums are available for online sharing almost immediately after release and in some cases, such as Oasis and Eminem, even before. Copy protection technology has been ineffective.

The development of broadband facilitates music sharing. A soundtrack that takes more than 12 minutes to download with a dial-up connection can be downloaded in as little as 20 seconds with a high-speed connection. Napster and its successors were banned in many universities because the very fast connections apparently induced so much file sharing that there was little available bandwidth left for anything else. In the case of the University of Illinois at Urbana-Champaign, this amounted to 75 percent of the total bandwidth.

File sharing is not limited to music. The development of fast connections is extending downloading to other digital goods such as movies, software, video games, and books. Some movies are available online during the opening week of theatrical release and before the authorized DVD is available.

Does file sharing reduce music sales? If so, what is the magnitude of the impact of file sharing on music sales? Is file sharing responsible for the recent drop in sales? Inside the music industry, it is generally accepted that music sales have been affected negatively by file sharing, but there has not been much empirical work done to measure the size and extent of this effect.

The question is important because file-sharing technology may undermine the effective protection offered by copyright.

Strong property rights create monopoly distortions, but weak property rights may lead to low levels of creation of artistic work or innovation. The balance between these opposing forces has rarely been empirically addressed. Knowledge of the impact of file sharing on sales is an essential part of the information needed for balancing these factors in the case of digital goods. . . .

The Music Industry

Global music sales in 2002 totaled US$32.2 billion. Forty-one percent of these sales were made in North America, 34.5 percent in Europe, 18.6 percent in Asia—with Japan representing more than 80 percent of Asian sales—3.1 percent in Latin America, and 2.7 percent distributed among Australasia, the Middle East, and Africa. Sales are concentrated in the top markets. The top five countries—the United States, Japan, the United Kingdom, France, and Germany—represent 76.5 percent of global sales, and the top 10—the top five above plus Canada, Italy, Spain, Australia, and Mexico—represent 85 percent.

Sales are also concentrated among a few companies. The four biggest companies—Universal, Sony-BMG, EMI, and Warner—control more than 70 percent of the global market of music sales, with the rest of the market share distributed among many independent record labels. These latter labels, in some cases, have an important presence in an individual country, region, or continent.

Companies and musicians usually negotiate exclusive multiyear contracts. When producing a new album, artists typically receive an up-front payment and a royalty somewhere between 5 and 13 percent of the retail price of the record.

The CD is the most popular music format, representing 72 percent of total international units sales. Sales of singles, LPs, and cassettes continue to be replaced by sales of CD albums. Two new formats, DVD Audio and Super Audio CD, are growing but do not yet have an important share. These new formats have higher sound quality and extra content such us video clips and interviews with the artists. The tendency to include extra content might have been accelerated by the need to differentiate the product from the illegal online substitute.

There is variability in prices across CDs. While the average retail price of a CD in the United States is US$14.19, 28 of the top 50 albums on the *Billboard* [magazine devoted to the music industry] charts have a list price between US$17.98 and US$19.98, and only seven are listed at US$14.98 or less. There is little information on music prices for other countries. In 2001, the European Commission [executive branch of the European Union] opened an investigation to study the higher prices in Europe and the divergence in prices inside the European Union. In 2003, the average price of a CD in the United Kingdom was US$16.80.

Distribution costs of music represent a very important share of total costs. A CD with a suggested price to consumers of US$16.98 has a price of US$10.50 to the retailer. This latter figure includes distribution costs from the record company to the retailer.

Music Stores: Shrinking as a Source

The distribution channels have been changing. Music stores have been shrinking as a source of sales and are being replaced by supermarkets, discount stores, department stores, and online retail. In the United States, music stores' share of sales fell from 62 percent in 1991 to 42 percent in 2000. In the United Kingdom, supermarkets increased their share of music sales from 11.2 percent in 1999 to 17.7 percent in 2001. Online retail (off-line delivery), as a share of total sales, increased from 6 percent in 2001 to 9 percent in 2002 in Germany and from 4 percent to 6 percent in the United Kingdom and remained steady at 3 percent in the United States. Online legitimate delivery became available in 2001, but it is still not an

". . . No Offense, but I downloaded all your music off the Internet. . . . . . None taken, I downloaded all your credit card info off the Internet. . . Wilson," cartoon by Dave Coverly. Used with permission of Dave Coverly and the Cartoonist Group. All rights reserved.

important source of sales. In 2003, sales of music downloads in the United States totaled US$30 million, which represents .25 percent of total music sales.

Online legitimate delivery and file sharing are possible in MP3 format. The MP3 format is a way to compress audio data without significantly compromising sound quality.

Sound recordings are originally represented as waves. When the sounds are digitalized, these waves are sampled many times per second and a file is created. Compact disc quality needs a sampling of 44,100 times per second (44.1 KHz). Humans can hear only around 10 percent of the sounds that are recorded on a CD. The MP3 compression system eliminates sounds that are not perceptible to humans and softer sounds when different sounds are playing simultaneously. There are different qualities of MP3 compression (depending on the bit rate of the file). Bit rates between 64 and 192 Kbps [kilobytes per second] are standard on the Internet, but only files above 160 Kbps have quality comparable to CDs.

A 5-minute soundtrack that would take more than 50 MB [megabytes] in CD compression format can be reduced to a file of 5 MB without significantly affecting the sound quality. A compressed file of this size can be downloaded in as fast as 12 minutes with a dial-up Internet connection (56 Kbps modem downstream), 1 minute and 20 seconds with a regular DSL [digital subscriber line] or cable connection (512 Kbps downstream), and 20 seconds with a fast DSL connection (2,000 Kbps downstream). However, the actual downloading speed also depends on the upstream speed connection of the computer providing the file, and the upstream speed is usually lower than the downstream speed.

People can upload (rip) CDs to their PCs' hard drives and listen to music on their computer, compress the files to an MP3 format to reduce the storage memory requirement and to facilitate the sharing of the files over the Internet, and convert the files back to a CD format and burn CDs that can be played in a regular player. The development of these technologies could represent a very significant reduction in costs considering that around 50 percent of music costs are distribution expenses.

Overshadowed by Piracy

There are many alternatives for getting music online. They can be divided into two groups: legitimate and illegitimate (under the current law).

Legitimate companies either own the copyright or make deals with copyright owners to distribute their music. Among the biggest companies are iTunes, [legal, revamped] Napster, Rhapsody, and the Europe-based OD2. Most services offer unlimited "streaming audio" and "tethered downloads" for a fixed charge per month of around US$10 and the possibility of permanent burnable downloads for around US$1 per song. In 2003, prices of digital tracks in Europe were higher, between US$1.76 and US$2.35 per song (Koranteng 2003), but they have decreased in the past 2 years.

Online legitimate digital delivery has been overshadowed by piracy. After the shutdown of Napster, illegitimate music online can still be found globally on peer-to-peer file-sharing services such as Kazaa, BitTorrent, and several others. These services are distributed without charge and allow users to download both licensed and unlicensed files, including music, movies, games, and software. The amount of music available through these services is larger than on any legitimate site.

Since the second half of 2003, the RIAA [Recording Industry Association of America] has been suing individual users who are offering substantial amounts of copyrighted music over peer-to-peer networks. The industry claims that these lawsuits are behind the leveling off of the decline in U.S. music sales in 2004. . . .

An Increasingly Important Issue

Global music sales have experienced a large drop. . . . Using measures of Internet sophistication as instruments, downloads may explain a 30 percent reduction in the probability of buying music.

The estimates in this paper are an important component of any welfare analysis of file sharing or copyright. The interest is not exclusive to the music industry. Other digital copyrighted goods such as movies, software, games, and books are also being shared online. The development of fast connections is likely to increase the impact of file sharing on sales of these goods. This is going to become an increasingly important issue in the next few years.

Downloading copyrighted material is illegal under the current legal system. The music industry is fighting file sharing in court. In the United States, music piracy has been legally fought on the basis of contributory and vicarious liability. Under these doctrines, copyright holders sue parties that in some way contribute to or benefit from the infringing conduct, instead of suing individuals. However, the new peer-to-peer systems have proven to be more difficult to fight legally because they do not require a central server to operate and have alternative legitimate uses. The other difficulty is that many of these new systems are established in countries with different legal systems: Kazaa is registered in the South Pacific island nation of Vanuatu, the software distributor is in Australia, and the servers are in the Netherlands.

After running into difficulties shutting down file-sharing systems, the RIAA changed strategy and has been "gathering evidence and preparing lawsuits against individual computer users who are illegally offering large amounts of copyrighted music over peer-to-peer networks." In Europe, the industry started suing individuals only in the middle of 2004.

There is controversy about the effect of this strategy on the number of downloads. While suing individuals who offer music—as opposed to individuals who download files—may reduce the number of files available to download, it is not clear whether this would actually affect the number of downloads. This is important when considering the public-good nature of the files offered online. In addition, while it appears that the number of users has decreased for some popular sites such as Kazaa, the legal strategy appears to have induced individuals to use alternative and less popular sites and forums where the risk of being prosecuted may be lower. The music industry claims that the recovery of sales that occurred in the United States in 2004 may be explained by the success of the new legal strategy.

"The history of media innovation for the last hundred years is essentially a history of gadgets that have been considered at one time or another to be 'pirate' technologies."

File-Sharing Copyrighted Media Helps to Advance Technology

Ken Hunt

In the following viewpoint, Ken Hunt claims that technologies that initially enable piracy lead to significant innovations in the way movies, music, and other media are distributed and consumed. For example, the author contends that the film industry's slowness to embrace the efficiency of movie downloads recalls its sky-is-falling claims about the videocassette recorders, which gave way to highly profitable movie rentals. Moreover, Hunt proposes that consumers will pay for services that give them more choices, better quality, and greater convenience than piracy provides. Ken Hunt writes for the Globe and Mail, *a Toronto-based Canadian newspaper.*

Ken Hunt, "Don't Fear the Pirates," *Globe and Mail*, November 27, 2007. Copyright © 2007 Globe Interactive, a division of Bell Globemedia Publishing, Inc. Reproduced by permission.

As you read, consider the following questions:

1. How does Daniel Defoe's story support Hunt's argument for piracy?

2. According to the author, how has software piracy helped Microsoft achieve market dominance?

3. How will Google Book Search help authors, in Hunt's view?

In 1701, Daniel Defoe wrote the satirical poem The True-Born Englishman, and it was a sensation. It was the best-selling poem of its day, but a large number of those sales didn't put any money into Defoe's pockets. This was a shame, became Defoe really could have used the cash. He had had money problems for a long time and was just managing to climb out of a bankruptcy as an estimated 80,000 unauthorized copies of his poem were being distributed. As far as we know, the people who made those copies and sold them in the streets are the first intellectual property thieves in history ever to be referred to as "pirates."

As charged with meaning as the word "pirate" is today, it held a bit more power in Defoe's time: 1701 was also the year that Captain Kidd was tried and hanged in London for murder and piracy on the high seas. His body was placed in a steel cage and hung over the Thames for two years as a warning to other would-be pirates. (Obviously the Recording Industry Association of America has nothing on the English Crown when it comes to intimidation.)

Defoe, however, was not very upset by the piracy of his work. In 1703, he published a corrected edition of the famous poem, and in the preface he wrote: "I should have been concerned at its being printed again and again by pirates, as they call them, and paragraph-men; but would that they do it justice and print it true according to the copy, they are welcome to sell it for a penny if they please."

Even though the pirates hadn't made Defoe rich, they had done him a huge favour: They made his words available to the general public much more cheaply than the publishing monopolies of the day would allow. This wide readership helped establish his literary reputation, making him one of the most famous men in England and assuring that his future works would find an audience. Even the King befriended him. For much of the rest of his life, Defoe would refer to himself simply as the author of The True-Born Englishman.

There's a lot we can learn from Defoe's example. While it's definitely not right that someone should have their intellectual property stolen or used without their permission—especially so that someone else can profit off of it—history teaches us that we generally stand to gain as much from piracy as we stand to lose. Yet almost without exception, movie, software, recording and publishing companies are gripped by an irrational fear of piracy that leads them to make decisions that are bad for their customers and, ultimately, destructive to themselves.

The history of media innovation for the last hundred years is essentially a history of gadgets that have been considered at one time or another to be "pirate" technologies. Time after time, these technologies have been opposed by the status quo and embraced by consumers. In each case the consumers have won, and in each case the more efficient and convenient distribution of media has been a financial boon to the industry as a whole.

Born of Piracy

The Motion Picture Association of America (MPAA) has been among the most vocal proponents of extending copyright laws and expanding the powers of law enforcement to track down file-sharers. Yet, one doesn't have to look very far back to discover that the motion picture industry itself was born of piracy—and we're not just talking about Errol Flynn movies. In fact, the primary reason that the movie industry settled in southern California was so that it could be beyond the reach of Thomas Edison and his patent lawyers. In the early years of the 20th century, Edison controlled almost all of the patents for movie-making technologies, including raw film. But Edison was headquartered in New Jersey, and across the country in California, movie makers could pirate his inventions with little fear of reprisal.

By the time the law caught up with Hollywood, Edison's patents had expired or been cancelled by the U.S. Supreme Court, and the movie industry was thriving.

Perhaps being born of piracy itself, the movie industry is particularly susceptible to fears that other pirates will come along and rob them of their booty. When video-cassette recorders were first introduced, the movie industry feared for its life. According to the industry, not only did VCRs destroy the movie experience by taking it from the big screen to the small one, they also enabled rampant piracy. Universal sued Sony, claiming that the company should be held liable for enabling the copyright infringement of its users. Universal lost, and the right of consumers to tape programs off of television for their own personal use was enshrined in law. Eventually, of course, the movie industry came to embrace the technology, and movie rentals wound up becoming—and remain—a major profit centre for the industry.

Today, the MPAA is suing BitTorrent companies like Vancouver-based IsoHunt.com. BitTorrent is the technology that massively improves the download speed for large files by grabbing small pieces of the file from many users at once. A two-hour movie can typically be downloaded via BitTorrent on a regular high-speed home connection in under an hour. As bandwidth improves, that time will only shrink.

Gary Fung is the 24-year-old CEO of IsoHunt, a company he started in 2002, when he was a first-year engineering student at the University of British Columbia. The company does not store any copyright-protected material on its servers; all it does is enable people who want to download and share large files of any type to find one another. They don't provide the software that makes the download possible or the software that plays downloaded movie files, but the MPAA argues that merely keeping a searchable list of where users can find files is an inducement to infringement. Never mind that much of the same information could also be found on Google simply by searching for "filetype:torrent." Fung maintains that his search engine, like Google, is agnostic to content and that there's no way to monitor the content users might be sharing. He also points out that, like YouTube, when IsoHunt receives a request to remove a link to a particular piece of copyright-protected material, the company honours those requests in a timely fashion.

Still, he believes that the movie industry is wrong in its approach to technology. "The VCR transitioned entertainment from the theatre to people's homes," says Fung. "The Internet will bring immediate and global distribution that's cheaper than ever and is the natural next step." There's no doubt that Fung is right about that. BitTorrent technology should have been recognized immediately by the movie studios as a way to make their distribution chain more efficient. But the industry was so locked in its old business model that they allowed an entire culture of free movie-sharing to evolve with no reasonable, legal alternative.

Stunning Efficiency

A classic example of the stunning efficiency of "pirate" technologies may come as high-definition movies start to be distributed by BitTorrent. The format wars between HD DVD and Blu-ray could quickly become a historical footnote if, instead of trying to stuff all that high-def data onto a little round disk, movie studios decided that it could easily be distributed on the Internet. These files would be very large—

"Yeah! I've got some anti-piracy software we can embed in our next music cd. Er, what does it cost? Nothing. I pirated it off the internet." cartoon by Adrian Raeside. Used with permission of Adrian Raeside and the Cartoonist Group. All rights reserved.

somewhere on the order of 20 GB [gigabytes] or more—and at current speeds could take a full day to download, but bandwidth speed is increasing all the time, and this could become a reality very soon. Billions were spent on the development of HD DVD and Blu-ray. The development of BitTorrent, in contrast, was largely supported by PayPal donations to the developer, Bram Cohen.

Cable television provides a perfect example of how the embrace of a supposedly "pirate" technology can change an industry. Cable TV started life as a "community antennae" that was capable of pulling in broadcasts from far greater distances than were possible with a regular roof antennae or a set of rabbit ears. Local broadcasters saw this as an immediate threat and launched lawsuits. In the end, not only did cable win out, it managed to create a market for a paid subscription service where a free service had existed in the past.

Those who fear that today's youth are being trained that music or movies can be had for free would be wise to consider the cable subscription model. Consumers are willing to abandon free services if a new technology can give them more choice, better quality and greater convenience.

The music industry, of course, has always been slow to embrace new technology. Any time someone makes a technological advance, the recording industry claims that the sky is falling. They claimed that cassette tapes would kill the industry because of the ease of copying. Instead, cassettes allowed music to move into cars, portable stereos and, eventually, the Walkman. This vastly increased the number of ways that customers could consume music. The industry was also wrong about digital audio tapes, and they were certainly wrong about MP3s. While they claim that downloads are destroying the business, every indication is that they're wrong. Concert sales, ringtones and digital downloads are all on their way up. It's only CD sales that are down, and those are only down about the same amount as they were in the years following the disco bust.

Soon the music industry will have to realize that selling music on CDs is just a bad business model. Taking digital information, burning it onto a piece of plastic, wrapping that in several more layers of plastic, shipping it across the country to suburban malls, which customers are then expected to drive to so their musical taste can be sneered at by an 18-year-old sales clerk, is just not a system that makes sense any more. It's the difference between snail mail and e-mail.

The Best Marketing Tool

You'd expect the technology-savvy people in the software industry to be a little smarter when it comes to balancing convenience and the risks of piracy, but Microsoft would prove you wrong. The company has spent millions on the Microsoft Genuine Advantage program to crack down on pirated copies of Vista and XP. All this, despite the fact that Microsoft would probably not have attained its dominance without software pirates. In the developing world, pirated copies of Windows are far more common than legitimate ones, but as happens in North America, illegitimate users are gradually being converted to legitimate users as they upgrade. Pirated Windows is easily the best marketing tool that Microsoft has ever had. Jeff Raikes, the president of Microsoft's business group, recently admitted as much, at [the 2007] Morgan Stanley Technology conference in San Francisco. "If they're going to pirate somebody, we want it to be us rather than somebody else," Raikes told the crowd.

What's true for Microsoft is also true for other expensive software packages, such as Adobe Photoshop. Why would someone pay $700 for a software package they'll only use to edit family photos, when pirated copies of Photoshop are easy to find, and it's the industry standard? Plus, as teenagers with an interest in design grow up using the software, it's the only thing they'd want to use if they became professional designers. There's no room for a cheaper, inferior piece of software in the marketplace, so nothing else can gain significant market share.

As we know from Defoe's example, the publishing industry has been dealing with pirates longer than anyone else. New technologies, from cheaper presses to photocopiers to optical text recognition, have continuously threatened them, and the pirating of books remains a real problem to this day. Despite hundreds of years of legal work and international conventions that protect the rights of authors and publishers, in many parts of the world, it's easier to find a pirated copy of a Harry Potter book than it is to find the real thing.

Perhaps no technology strikes as much fear into the hearts of some publishers as does Google's book-scanning efforts. The search giant announced the program at the Frankfurt Book Fair in 2004, and so far they have already scanned over a million titles into their database. The full text of The True-Born Englishman hasn't made it onto the site yet, but at least Defoe's Robinson Crusoe [his most famous work] is there.

A search on the text of that book finds the first mention of pirates on page 20—the real kind this time. Google claims that the tool will help customers find what they want and ultimately help publishers sell more books. But as with the music industry, publishers fear that once information becomes digital, it's easy to lose control of it.

Meghann Marco, author of Field Guide to the Apocalypse, is someone who recognizes that obscurity is a much greater threat to the livelihood of a writer than piracy. Much of her day is spent trying to drum up attention for her book, and she was excited by the possibility of it being included in Google Book Search. Marco's publisher, Simon & Schuster, on the other hand, told her that that would not be happening. They're part of the Association of American Publishers, which is suing Google for copyright infringement.

Marco sent a letter of support to Google, which quickly made its way around the Internet. In it, she tells a story of being challenged by someone about giving away her work for free. "What if someone Xeroxed your book and was handing it out for free on street corners?" the person asked her.

Marco's reply: "Well, it seems to be working for Jesus."

> "Large software vendors, who stand to lose tens of millions of dollars annually to software pirates often conduct their own educational programs, warning that counterfeit software is not only illegal, but can damage a corporate PC—a loss the company must then replace."

Copyright Infringement of Software Has Serious Consequences

Frank Washkuch Jr.

Frank Washkuch Jr. "has been online editor of SC Magazine *since November 2005." In the following viewpoint, Washkuch recounts efforts by Chinese law enforcement authorities to apprehend software pirates and counterfeiters. Washkuch then discusses statistics that show financial gains from legal software use and losses in revenue from pirated software use. Washkuch uses Microsoft as an example of a company that must deal with pirated software on a large scale and that combats piracy through cooperation with law enforcement and through education of the*

Frank Washkuch Jr., "Against Piracy: While Pirated Software Is Common in Many Countries, Steps Are Being Taken to Halt the Practice," *SC Magazine*, vol. 18, no. 10, October 2007, pp. 35(3). Copyright © 2007 Haymarket Media, Inc. Reproduced by permission.

public on the illegality of piracy as well as on the dangers of pi-
rated software to PCs. Washkuch also points out that software
piracy tends to occur more in small to medium size businesses
than in large businesses.

As you read, consider the following questions:

1. What two countries, according to Washkuch, have been
   the source of much counterfeiting?

2. How much revenue was lost to copyright owners in
   2006 through the installation of pirated software?

3. According to Washkuch, what is the reason why large
   busniesses are less likely to use pirated software than
   smaller companies?

When Chinese law enforcement authorities in July
rounded up members of two criminal organizations allegedly responsible for $500 million in counterfeit software, it
was hailed by the FBI and software vendors as a considerable
blow to high quality Chinese counterfeiters.

The 25 arrests, which included Ma Kei Pei—indicted in
the U.S. in 2003 before fleeing to China for allegedly creating
fake Microsoft programs—represent the first results of an increased anti-piracy partnership between U.S. and Chinese authorities. Such a working relationship is no small matter when
dealing with a country long regarded as the world's prime
source of illegally copied goods, but now widely regarded as
trying to whitewash its image before the 2008 Olympic Games
in Beijing.

For U.S.-based software vendors, the arrests were good
news for numerous reasons. The break-up of a piracy syndicate results in less fake merchandise on the streets, but it is
also a symbolic victory, signaling likely future busts, says Chris
Paden, public relations manager at Symantec, a company
whose software Ma Kei Pei is accused of replicating.

"When Ma and other members of his syndicate were arrested, not a lot of the recovered products were Symantec, but

we helped authorities in terms of information. Bringing down that syndicate was a big step," he says. "I think that was a very big step that was very encouraging for many people over here. It was encouraging that the FBI and Chinese law enforcement worked together."

While the arrests may have only dented the armor of worldwide piracy, other data suggests that the rates of piracy in countries such as China and Russia—hotbeds of counterfeiting of all kinds—have taken a hit in recent years. A study released in May by the Business Software Alliance (BSA), a nonprofit which fosters copyright protection, cyber security, trade and e-commerce, and conducted by IDC, revealed that the rate of pirated software has decreased by 10 percent in China over the past three years. In Russia, the piracy rate dropped by seven percentage points over the same period of time. Contrary to these trends, the legitimate software market in China grew to $1.2 billion in 2006, an increase of 88 percent from the year before, and a jump of 358 percent from 2003.

But not all of the percentages in the BSA survey signal positive developments. More than $100 billion in pirated software was installed on PCs in 2006 and the global piracy rate for that year was 35 percent, the same as 2005, according to the BSA.

Efforts Are Paying Off

Large enterprises and organizations such as the BSA, which have an international reach and can lobby foreign governments, can take the statistics as a sign that their efforts are paying off. However, much work must be done to pressure foreign governments to increase anti-piracy regulations, says Rodger Correa, BSA compliance marketing director.

"What we are doing is working with governments, and governments can do a lot to reduce software piracy," he says. "A lot has to do with government control. An example is re-

User, Not Owner

When you purchase software, you do not become the owner of the copyright. Rather, you are purchasing the right to use the software under certain restrictions imposed by the copyright owner, typically the software publisher. The precise rules are described in the documentation accompanying the software—the license. It is imperative that you understand and adhere to these rules. . . . Even if you only help someone else make unauthorized copies, you are still liable under the copyright law.

Business Software Alliance,
"Software Piracy and the Law: Information on Software Piracy
in the United States," www.bsa.org, (Accessed October 2008).

ducing China's piracy rate by 10 percent. There are positives, but there is much more to be done."

No software vendor feels the heat of pirate activity as much as Microsoft, whose operating systems and applications run on the vast majority of home and corporate computers around the world. Because software pirates rely on name recognition to sell counterfeit goods, Microsoft has an unusually large target on its back. In response, the software giant takes a three-pronged approach to fending off piracy, says Michael Beare, director, channel, Genuine Software Initiative at Microsoft. This strategy includes educating the public on the dangers of software piracy, using technical advances, such as the Windows Genuine Advantage program, and also working with law enforcement authorities, according to Beare.

"We have a really strong legal team comprised of attorneys supporting the U.S. Customs and Border Patrol and trying to detect the counterfeit products," he says. "That's investment that has been distracted away from bettering our products."

Large software vendors, who stand to lose tens of millions of dollars annually to software pirates often conduct their own educational programs, warning that counterfeit software is not only illegal, but can damage a corporate PC—a loss the company must then replace. The use of pirated software tends to be more common in small- and medium-sized businesses (SMB) because of a lack of attention. The emergence of the Sarbanes-Oxley Act of 2002 as a regulatory tool has minimized the use of pirated software in larger corporations, says Correa.

"Most piracy tends to be concentrated in SMBs. We do realize that SMBs are working with limited resources, and software resources sometimes aren't at the top of their priorities. In the past, it was also concentrated in larger corporations, but with the influx of SOX, that has been reduced in the past couple years," he says. "We have done quite a bit of advertising and quite a bit of communications overall. I would be surprised if companies weren't aware of us."

Another obstacle facing legitimate software vendors is that the bad guys sometimes have a technical advantage. The key to unlocking and reverse-engineering software is sometimes just a few web searches away, says Michael Dager, CEO of Arxan, a leading provider of intellectual property protection designed to prevent software piracy.

"The bigger problem is that the hackers and the pirates, themselves sophisticated programmers, have jumped in a major way in front of the software vendors and the license management vendors," he says. "The proliferation of hacking tools, things like reverse compilers, has increased exponentially over the past couple of years, and the quantity of tools and the methodology of these tools has leapt ahead."

Don't Step on Toes

In addition, software companies must keep in mind another group of people when trying to fend off pirates—their own customers. A technical anti-piracy solution should stay off the toes of end-users while protecting the company's intellectual property, says Gord Larose, senior application security engineer at Cloakware, a Vienna, Va.-based security solutions provider.

"I think there's certainly room for technology, but you have to strike a careful balance between something that's bulletproof and annoys people," says Larose.

While there are other methods to fight piracy other than handcuffs and police raids, the effectiveness of working with law enforcement authorities shouldn't be underestimated. Investigative units are used by many large vendors to follow the tracks of criminals benefitting from the sale of counterfeit software. Combined with technical precautions and public education—as well as the awareness efforts of other organizations—this can make for an effective piracy fighting program, says Scott Minden, director of legal affairs, Symantec.

"We're going to continue our current course, which is aggressive investigations and continuing to publicize this as best we can," says Minden. "We want to really let the pirates know that we're after them, and to let consumers know that we're focusing on what they purchase. One thing we'd really like to focus on is increasing our education drive to the public."

> "The subject of software piracy, it seems, isn't as straightforward as it might appear."

Some Believe the Piracy of Copyrighted Software May Have Benefits

Network World

In the following viewpoint, the author suggests that software piracy, though broadly condemned by major software vendors such as Microsoft and IBM, has supporters. According to the author, some open source software advocates argue that piracy benefits users. In addition, the author suggests that some previously cash-strapped companies have been able to create innovative products and contribute to economic growth by pirating expensive software. Network World *is a weekly information technology publication based in Framington, Massachusetts.*

As you read, consider the following questions:

1. What are the Business Software Alliance's figures for software piracy rates in the United States and China, according to *Network World*?

Network World, "Software Piracy: Love It or Hate It," July 10, 2006, p. 19. All contents copyright © 1995–2008 Network World, Inc. Reproduced by permission.

2. Why does critic Michael Masnick oppose the "lost sale" argument, according to *Network World*?

3. What practices does *Network World* recommend to prevent software piracy?

Big vendors such as Microsoft and IBM say that they're collectively losing billions of dollars a year in software sales because of piracy, and are working together and with government to address the problem. But others argue that the problem is overblown and that piracy has its place in the industry.

The subject of software piracy, it seems, isn't as straightforward as it might appear.

Software piracy has been broadly condemned by large vendors, particularly through their participation in the Business Software Alliance (BSA). The BSA's goal is to protect intellectual property and prevent individuals or companies from pirating or counterfeiting commercial software. The BSA has claimed some success in North America, where the percentage of pirated software hovers at about 22% though the alliance faces a much bigger challenge in other parts of the world, such as China, where it says 86% of software was pirated [in 2005].

The U.S. government also has been targeting piracy. Led by [then-]Attorney General Alberto Gonzalez, the Department of Justice . . . stepped up efforts by its intellectual property task force, which was instituted in 2004. The Justice Department [as of 2005 had] 25 Computer Hacking and Intellectual Property units across the United States that investigate intellectual property crimes.

Software customers also are speaking out. "We've seen the costs of software rise over the last several years," says Michael Sherwood, CIO [chief information officer] for the city of Oceanside, Calif. "We attribute that or a portion of that cost increase to piracy."

Not Everyone

But not everyone holds the opinion that software piracy is bad. Some open source advocates, for example, bristle at the likening of someone who makes a copy of licensed software for someone else to a pirate. Open source guru Richard Stallman, who founded the Free Software Foundation, once said: "Helping your neighbor is not piracy; piracy is attacking ships."

A ... posting on the Techdirt blog by Michael Masnick, president and CEO [chief executive office] of the independent corporate intelligence firm, sums up the criticism of the BSA's method of estimating the financial damages from software piracy. In the posting, he called the BSA's yearly software-piracy findings "bogus," because the BSA says every unauthorized copy is a "lost sale." Masnick's argument is that if someone isn't going to buy it, he isn't going to buy it, legal copy or not.

Further, pirated software helps some companies with tight budgets create innovative products and contribute to the overall U.S. economy, Masnick wrote.

Indeed, one IT [information technology] support manager for a software company who asked not to be named says her company's product, which now is widely used in a niche market, would not exist if it had not been for software piracy.

Before being acquired by a larger organization, the company would send one licensed copy of server software to multiple locations, because it could not afford to purchase as many licenses as it needed to develop its product, she says. The company was eventually charged with software piracy, but its product was purchased by a larger company and is now extremely successful, she says.

"I wouldn't be where I was today without software piracy," she says.

Nevertheless, software customers say they aren't taking any chances with pirated software. "We're acutely aware that software piracy is the same thing as theft," says one IT manager at a global energy company, who asked not to be named. "It's not just intellectual property [at stake]; it's theft. We do everything we can short of just stopping the business [to prevent piracy]."

These efforts include regularly sweeping servers to search for files and programs that don't belong on them. The company also recently updated its Microsoft System Management Server environment to provide much better reporting about what applications are running on the network, the IT manager says.

The organization also makes it easy for anyone with budgetary approval to buy software for people if they think it is necessary for them to do their job. "We lower the threshold for people getting the software they need," he says, pointing out that this lessens the incentive for illegally copying software.

Oceanside's Sherwood says his organization is so careful about the software it runs in-house that even if an employee buys software legally, the software will be ripped out if the city hasn't approved it.

Not Always as Easy

The BSA, which estimates North American software companies lost $6.9 billion from software piracy [in 2005], recommends that software customers help fight piracy just by keeping track of their software.

"The most important thing a network administrator can do is know what is on his or her own network and know what he or she has bought," says Jenny Blank, director of enforcement at the BSA.

This is not always as easy as it sounds, especially with large organizations. Marcel Warmerdam, an IDC [Interactive Data Corporation] analyst, suggests using asset-management software, which is available for big-name companies and lesser-known ones.

Copyright Law—An Old Bottle

On the proprietary software side, a multitude of forces are amassed against would-be, so-called software "pirates", which probably tarnishes a large portion of the population in general. We have copyright law—an old bottle, arguably not well tailored to house this new wine—but chosen in the 1980s as an appropriate legal protection for a number of reasons, including the fact that it was considered a good idea to treat software code in the same way as you would treat a literary work. Signatories to the Berne Convention [an international treaty on copyright involving many countries, including the United States] could provide this protection almost instantaneously and, therefore, a rapid, international coverage for software was achieved.

Copyright is not the same in all countries so software owners get a bundle of rights rather than a single one that will suffice in every jurisdiction. Moreover, proprietary software licences tend to restrict these rights, in return for permission to use the work in a limited way. Copy protection is also used in tandem with copyright law and this creates a physical fence to keep software "thieves" and other miscreants out. Despite the copyright bargain of leaving ideas free while protecting expression, patent law has subsequently been applied to this material, which was supposed to lie in the public domain. Industry representative bodies, such as the Business Software Alliance, are fond of pointing out the humungous losses caused by "pirates" and they have developed a moral arsenal of a type of online confessional by proxy where disgruntled employees are encouraged to report their errant bosses.

Maureen O'Sullivan, "A Law for Free Software: Don't We Have Enough Laws Already?" Free Software Magazine, April 3, 2005.

"The advantage is two-way," he says. "It identifies what software there is and how much it is used."

However, the IT manager for the global energy company says asset-management software is difficult and expensive to install and maintain, and so might not be a viable option for every organization.

"I know companies that have spent an enormous amount of money trying to get a handle on it," he says. "Sometimes it would be easier to buy a lot of extra copies [of software] and hand them out than try to count them all."

The BSA offers a set of free tools and resources online that can help organizations enact policies and best practices to prevent software piracy, and train employees in the legal ramifications of pirating software.

Best practices for preventing software piracy

- Install an asset-management program to identify your software resources and how often they are used.

- If asset-management software is not an option, regularly audit the software resources on your network to identify what software you have and where it came from.

- Make it easy for managers and IT decision makers to free up financial resources for software if they find it is necessary for the organization; employees won't pirate software if they can just as easily purchase it.

- Educate employees on the legal responsibilities and ramifications that exist if they pirate software.

- Implement a companywide policy for how to deal with employees who pirate software.

> *"The loss of intellectual property rights and the proliferation of counterfeit goods not only cost American jobs, they pose serious safety risks to the American people."*

Counterfeit Goods Hurt the Economy

Joe Knollenberg

In the following viewpoint, Joe Knollenberg contends that the flood of counterfeit goods poses a serious threat to the U.S. economy, costing legitimate companies billions of dollars a year and Americans thousands of jobs. Although counterfeits are often nearly identical to the real thing, the author also maintains that knockoffs such as automobile parts and prescription drugs compromise the safety of unknowing consumers. Therefore, Knollenberg supports the stiff penalties that the Stop Counterfeiting in Manufactured Goods Act, enacted in 2006, places on counterfeiters. Joe Knollenberg was a Republican member of the U.S. House of Representatives from Michigan's 9th congressional district from 1993 to 2009.

Joe Knollenberg, "Testimony for the U.S. China Economic & Security Review Commission Hearing on Intellectual Property Rights Issues and Counterfeit Goods," June 8, 2006. www.uscc.gov. Reproduced by permission.

As you read, consider the following questions:

1. What figures does Knollenberg provide to support his claim that counterfeits damage the U.S. economy?

2. According to the author, why are differences in counterfeits almost impossible to detect?

3. In what ways does the Stop Counterfeiting Goods Act help combat counterfeiting, in Knollenberg's opinion?

Good morning everyone, and thank you for having me here today. I am extremely encouraged by the [U.S. China Economic and Security Review] Commission's hearings this week [June 2006] on intellectual property rights and counterfeit goods. The loss of intellectual property rights and the proliferation of counterfeit goods not only cost American jobs, they pose serious safety risks to the American people.

As you probably know, I represent a congressional district in suburban Detroit whose economy is largely centered around the auto industry. Daimler-Chrysler's North American headquarters is in my district, and a quarter of the top one-hundred of the largest auto suppliers in North America are headquartered in my district. This includes Robert Bosch's North American headquarters, Delphi, and Arvin-Meritor. Overall, I have over 1,500 manufacturing entities, and 92% have less than 100 employees.

I was particularly struck by the impact counterfeiters were having on the auto supplier industry. I knew counterfeiting was a problem, but I didn't realize the extent of the problem until countless companies made the effort to educate me about it.

What I learned was that counterfeit parts and goods cost American jobs. Counterfeit automobile parts cost the automotive supplier industry over $12 billion annually. It's estimated that if these losses were eliminated, the auto industry could hire 200,000 additional workers.

When it comes to the economy overall, the U.S. Customs Service has estimated that counterfeiting has resulted in the loss of 750,000 jobs and costs the United States around $200 billion annually. The International Chamber of Commerce estimates that seven percent of the world's trade is in counterfeit goods and that the counterfeit market is worth $350 billion.

It's important to remember these numbers, because counterfeiting is not a victimless crime. In addition to selling bogus products, the counterfeiters are stealing jobs and money away from legitimate companies.

Compromising Safety

Counterfeit parts not only damage our economy, they compromise the safety of all Americans. Counterfeit auto parts, such as fake tail-lights and brake pads, have been found being installed in New York City taxi cabs. Knockoffs to popular prescription drugs, such as Lipitor, have been confiscated and are nearly identical to the real thing. We have even heard of reports that counterfeit parts have been unintentionally installed in military combat vehicles.

Often times, there is virtually no way of telling the difference between a legitimate product and the counterfeit. Much of this can be attributed to the fact that counterfeiters have perfected everything—all the way down to the label and packaging—which I believe you have seen first-hand.

We must take a more aggressive stand against counterfeit parts. And one of the ways we are going to do that is to give the government more tools to fight counterfeiters.

To help accomplish this task, I introduced H.R. [House of Representatives bill] 32, the Stop Counterfeiting in Manufactured Goods Act. I was very pleased that President [George W.] Bush signed this bill into law [Spring 2006].

Before my bill was enacted, a convicted trademark counterfeiter was only required to give up the actual counterfeit goods. The problem was, the criminals could just turn right around and make more. In order to stop the counterfeiters, the consequences have to go further.

That is why H.R. 32 includes a provision that establishes mandatory destruction, forfeiture, and restitution provisions in trademark law—similar to those already in copyright law. This change is necessary to get at the roots of the problem.

Further, my bill would require the convicted criminals to give up not just the counterfeit goods, but also the equipment they used to make those goods. Seizing and destroying the equipment used to make counterfeit goods is necessary to put the criminals out of business.

In addition, the bill prohibits trafficking in counterfeit labels, patches, and medallions that are not necessarily attached to a particular counterfeit good. Before, it was legal to make and sell these items if they were not attached to a particular counterfeit good. This just didn't make sense. Why would counterfeiters make these labels, if not for the chance at illegal profits?

A Profound Impact

These simple changes will have a profound impact in combating counterfeit manufactured goods in many different ways.

H.R. 32 sends a signal to counterfeiters that the United States is serious about combating this growing problem. The enactment of this bill gives prosecutors more tools to go after the criminals here in the U.S. and punish them severely.

The bill is also necessary to address the problem globally. A large part of the counterfeit auto parts are coming from other countries, particularly China. So we need our trade negotiators to demand that our trading partners have strong anti-counterfeiting provisions.

But U.S. negotiators can't demand that other countries take steps to combat trademark counterfeiting unless we are taking those same steps ourselves. So, by enacting my bill and

Summary Table of Drivers for Counterfeit and Pirate Activities

Counterfeit or pirate supply	Knowing demand for counterfeit or pirated products
Driving factors	Driving factors
Market characteristics	Product characteristics
High unit profitability	Low prices
Large potential market size	Acceptable perceived quality
Genuine brand power	Ability to conceal status
Production, distribution and technology	Consumer characteristics
Moderate need for investments	No health concerns
Moderate technology requirements	No safety concerns
Unproblematic distribution and sales	Personal budget constraint
High ability to conceal operation	
Easy to decieve consumers	
Institutional characteristics	Institutional characteristics
Low risk of discovery	Low risk of discovery and prosecution
Legal and regulatory framework	Weak or no penalties
Weak enforcement	Availability and ease of acquisition
Non-deterrent penalties	Socio-economic factors

Organisation for Economic Co-operation and Development, "The Economic Impact of Counterfeiting and Piracy," 2007.

improving our own law, Congress has empowered our trade negotiators to press for stronger anti-counterfeiting provisions in other countries.

Passage of this bill also sends an important signal to our manufacturers here in America by demonstrating to them that the U.S. Congress is serious about improving the environment in which they compete by cracking down on the counterfeiters who cost them money, and cost Americans their jobs.

The International Anti-Counterfeiting Coalition, the U.S. Chamber of Commerce, the National Association of Manufacturers, the National Electrical Manufacturers Association, and a host of major corporations all supported H.R. 32. . . .

The size and scope of counterfeit manufactured goods around the world is growing every day. Legitimate manufacturers are making every reasonable effort they can to prevent it, but they could use some additional assistance from the federal government. That's what H.R. 32 will do.

"Estimates of the global trade in counterfeit goods are only as good as their underlying data."

The Statistics of Counterfeit Goods May Be Exaggerated

Felix Salmon

In the following viewpoint, Felix Salmon argues that recent counterfeit statistics for New York City, a hotspot for counterfeit and bootlegged goods, are implausible. According to him, the statistics, which report that the city looses $1 billion a year in tax revenues, are an exaggeration used for sensationalizing and scaremongering. While counterfeiting is a serious problem, the author maintains that misleading claims threaten the credibility of global estimates on the economic impacts of counterfeiting. Felix Salmon is a British writer living in New York.

As you read, consider the following questions:

1. Why is the claim that New Yorkers spent $23 billion on counterfeit goods not possible, according to Salmon?

2. What does Salmon mean when he says New York City comptroller William C. Thompson used a "top-down" approach to calculate his counterfeiting figures?

Felix Salmon, "Thompson's Counterfeit Numbers," *The New York Sun*, December 2, 2004. Copyright © 2004 *The New York Sun*, One SL, LLC. All rights reserved. Reproduced by permission.

3. Where do estimates on global counterfeiting originate, according to the author?

New York City Comptroller William C. Thompson Jr. does many things, but releasing reliable statistics is not one of them. In the week before Thanksgiving [2004], he released a report claiming that New York City is losing $1 billion a year in tax revenues due to trafficking in counterfeit trademark goods. He's the city comptroller, he should know, right? In fact, rather than reporting facts, he's exaggerating, sensationalizing, and scaremongering.

Mr. Thompson refuses to talk about his report. Instead, his office released a statement saying that their economists had consulted with unnamed "experts," and that "they, and we, stand by the numbers presented in the report."

Those numbers, however, aren't plausible. Take the first sentence of the report, which states that "New Yorkers paid $23 billion for counterfeit goods during 2003."

In fiscal 2004, New York City received $4 billion in sales tax revenue, which, at a sales tax rate of 8.625%, implies about $46 billion in total legal spending. If spending on counterfeit goods is indeed now $23 billion, then New York's black market would be fully half the size of its legitimate economy, accounting for a third of total spending.

No one, surely, lavishes a third of their total expenditure on fake goods. If the comptroller's estimates are right, then for every dollar you spent on hotels and restaurants, in bodegas [neighborhood markets] and department stores, in wine shops and music shops, on cars or bicycles or skateboards, you would, on average, spend 50 cents on counterfeit and bootlegged goods.

Mr. Thompson's numbers aren't even internally consistent. One would think that the unpaid sales tax on $23 billion in counterfeit goods would be about $2 billion, at the 8.625% rate. In fact, the comptroller says that unpaid sales tax on that $23 billion totals just $380 million, or 1.65%.

Good for Luxury Brands

Indeed, counterfeit products may be good for luxury brands. Because they are usually manufactured by lean, market-driven entrepreneurs, they are often the first signal of a luxury brand's renaissance (when copies appear) or of the final nail in the coffin (when they don't). As a result, more than one great luxury house uses counterfeit sales to predict demand for its own brand and gauge its overall health.

Mark Ritson, "Counterfeits: Good for Luxury Brands?"
Branding Strategy Insider, *October 3, 2007.*

So where is the comptroller getting his numbers? Not, it would seem, from any kind of on-the-ground legwork. The only breakdown of what the $23 billion is spent on comes at the end of the report, with an appendix on recorded music. There, we're told that in 2003, "approximately 17 million illicit sound recordings made their way undiscovered to the streets of New York City for sale to the public," generating some "$85 million in illicit sales per year." That $85 million accounts for roughly one-third of 1% of the $23 billion total: the other 99.63%, we can only assume, is "other."

Top-down, Not Bottom-up

In fact, Mr. Thompson works on a top-down, not a bottom-up, basis. He starts off by estimating global trade in counterfeit goods at $456 billion, or 6% of gross world trade. To back up that number, he cites the International Chamber of Commerce. Then, he estimates the size of the American counterfeit trade at $287 billion, leaving us to assume that somehow he's using the same estimate. He's not. In 2003, American goods exports were $714 billion and goods imports were $1,263 billion. Six percent of those two numbers is just $119 billion.

So where does the $287 billion figure—the basis for all the comptroller's subsequent calculations—come from? All the report says is that "this estimate is based upon an update of a 1996 estimate of U.S. losses," footnoting a 1996 article in Fortune magazine.

When you go to the article, it says that "federal and industry surveys indicate that America's annual losses from the problem have quadrupled over the past decade to a staggering $200 billion," without getting any more specific. It's the kind of pseudostatistic that is clearly a wild guess aimed more at scaring people than being accurate; what's more, it's [an old number]. But it's Mr. Thompson's best source for the size of the market for bootleg goods in New York.

The comptroller's "update" clearly consisted of adding $87 billion to that figure to make it seem like less of a round number. But even assuming that the $200 billion number was accurate and not exaggerated, there's a huge difference between losses and sales. If I sell a bootleg copy of Adobe's Creative Suite for $20, Adobe's loss is $1,200, while my sales are, well, $20.

It's a distinction, however, that seems lost on the comptroller. He says that New Yorkers are shelling out $23 billion in cash for counterfeit and bootlegged goods, and he's basing that figure not on sales estimates but on loss estimates. It's like counting the number of books in Barnes & Noble, and using that as an estimate for the total number of crime novels in stock.

Once he comes up with his spurious $287 billion number, Mr. Thompson then has to work out what New York's share of the national total is: In the end, he decides to do it by doubling the city's share. Nowhere does the comptroller explain why he's using a multiplier of two rather than 1.5, say, or even three or four or 10.

There's simply a bald statement: "The Comptroller's Office estimates that New York City's share of the U.S. counterfeit goods trade is twice its share of gross product." Not even a footnote, this time. Actually, none of the comptroller's estimates comes from New York data: All of them take broader numbers from the country or even the world as a whole and then work out what New York's share of that might be.

Hard to Credit

That is hard to credit. Estimates of the global trade in counterfeit goods are only as good as their underlying data, which necessarily must come from component states and municipalities. We're all for trying to block counterfeiting. It's a serious problem. But if the best that New York can do is to work down from the global estimates, rather than producing its own bottom-up analyses, then the main lesson that we can learn from the whole exercise is that none of these numbers really means anything at all.

Periodical Bibliography

Frank Ahrens — "Hollywood Says Piracy Has Ripple Effect," *Washington Post*, September 29, 2006.

Associated Press — "China's Piracy Hurting Its Own Industries," July 7, 2006.

Kayleigh Bateman — "Piracy Paves the Way," *Computer Reseller News*, February 18, 2008.

Susan Butler — "Casting the Net: The RIAA Provides an Inside Glimpse into Its Battle Against Illegal File Sharing," *Billboard*, June 14, 2008.

John C. Dvorak — "The Unintended Consequences of P2P Piracy," *PC Magazine*, March 19, 2007.

Economist — "Look for the Silver Lining," July 17, 2008.

Andrea Fuchs — "iCount . . . and iCatch You: Video Surveillance Enhances Fraud and Piracy Protection," *Film Journal International*, October 2008.

Heather Green and Susann Rutledge — "Does She Look Like a Music Pirate?" *Business Week*, May 5, 2008.

Matt Mason — "Pirates of the Third Screen," *Adweek*, February 25, 2008.

Ryan Sumo — "Piracy and the Underground Economy," *Escapist*, July 15, 2008.

Kathleen Tracy — "P2P No Longer Means Piracy 2 Everyone," *Video Age International*, September–October 2008.

Eric Wilson — "Fashion Industry Grapples with Designer Knockoffs," *International Herald Tribune*, September 4, 2007.

G. Pascal Zachary — "Piracy—The Price of Farm Subsidies," *San Francisco Chronicle*, December 11, 2005.

OPPOSING
VIEWPOINTS®
SERIES

CHAPTER 4

Are Copyright Laws Effective?

Chapter Preface

For many young, aspiring trendsetters, Forever 21 is the one-stop shop for high-fashion looks at low prices. Founded in 1984, the Los Angeles-based clothing retailer is a Fortune 500 company, with over 400 stores around the world. *Forbes Traveler* senior editor Jeff Koyen visited a Forever 21 outlet in America's fashion capital, New York City. "The knock-offs are easy to spot," he claimed, spying garments resembling the chic designs of Gucci and Marc Jacobs—at a fraction of their cost. But Seema Anand, whose apparel-manufacturing company is a vendor for Forever 21, maintains that she is inspired by, but does not copy, other designers. "We tweak it," Anand declares, adding that all style-conscious shoppers have the "right to look fabulous."

Forever 21's revenues broke $1 billion in 2006, thanks in part to its knack for making the latest trends accessible to the average consumer. But this template for success has racked up multiple lawsuits for the retailer. Designers Diane von Fürstenberg and Anna Sui, and singer Gwen Stefani, who owns clothing and effects brand Harajuku Lovers, have sued Forever 21 for lifting their designs and mass-producing runway-inspired frocks—sometimes before designers could take their bows. According to von Fürstenberg, as soon as fashion-show photos surface, they are immediately sent to copycat manufacturers, where "cheap versions of original designs" can be turned around within a day. Von Fürstenberg, president of the Council of Fashion Designers of America, is a proponent of the Design Piracy Prohibition Act. If signed into law, fashion designs would be copyrighted for three years. "We must protect American designers who are growing in their innovation and originality, emerging designs so they can flourish and, of course, the consumer," she says. In the 1970s, von Fürstenberg shifted her career into high gear with her signature wrap dress.

Detractors, however, suggest that the bill is counterproductive because designers constantly remake and revise existing designs. Executive director of the California Fashion Association Ilse Metchek asserts: "There is only so much you can do with a silhouette, a collar, a drape. For the little designers who have that one great idea and it's knocked off—well, welcome to the real world, guys. Make another one." Furthermore, others contend that even the most famed fashion houses reference others. Johnson Hartig, cofounder of the label Libertine, proposes, "Some of the biggest designers would be in court every other week for knocking off other people."

Forever 21 is a model business to admiring upstarts and fashionistas on a budget. On the other hand, industry foes view the retailer as a rogue purveyor of derivative, infringing fashions. In the following viewpoints, the authors debate this and other current issues in copyright laws.

> *"To preserve the moral and legal rights associated with authorship, it is essential that we credit and cite the ideas and creative works of those who inspire our own creative works."*

Copyright Laws Are Effective

Jennifer Horner

In the following viewpoint, Jennifer Horner contends that copyright laws provide safeguards to authors and creators of original works as well as fostering citizens' rights to learn and build upon the creativity of others. According to Horner, copyright laws differentiate novel ideas and creative expressions from common knowledge and allow the use of copyrighted works through attribution and the fair use doctrine. This provides enumeration and ownership rights to authors and creators while promoting intellectual growth and freedom without the threat of censorship, which the author claims is necessary in a free society. Jennifer Horner is an associate professor at the College of Health Professions at Medical University of South Carolina and holds a degree in law.

Jennifer Horner, "Understanding Copyright Law," *The ASHA Leader*, vol. 9, no. 16, September 7, 2004, pp. 6–7. Copyright © 2004 American Speech-Language-Hearing Association. Reproduced by permission of the publisher.

As you read, consider the following questions:

1. What does the author claim to be the purpose of the first copyright act?

2. How does the author summarize the difference between plagiarism and copyright infringement?

3. How is transferring copyright achieved, according to Horner?

Everyone can freely use the words in a language. One cannot steal "words," but one can steal another person's ideas and "creative forms of expression." That is why understanding copyright law is so important.

Safeguards are in place to protect authors, dating back to 1710 when the Statute of Anne was enacted in England. The world's first copyright act, this statute had a two-fold purpose: to respect the rights of authors in their original works and to abate censorship. In the United States, the Constitution first secured authors' rights in 1787. Additional protections came later in the U.S. Copyright Act of 1790 and the First Amendment to the Constitution in 1791.

Scope of the U.S. Copyright Act

The U.S. Copyright Act is found in Title 17 of the United States Code (USC)[i.e., federal law], and is available on the Library of Congress Web site. The Copyright Act has been amended numerous times (e.g., 1909, 1976), and was harmonized with the international Berne Convention for the Protection of Literary and Artistic Works in 1989 [a copyright treaty between over 150 countries, the Berne Convention is the closest thing there is to an international copyright law]. A 1998 amendment increased the term of copyright for literary works to the life of the author plus 70 years, while the Technology, Education and Copyright Harmonization Act of 2002 laid down special rules for digital media and distance education.

An Ethical Decision

But why respect copyright, especially if no one will ever know you "borrowed" someone else's copyright? It has to do with more than the probability of getting caught (or not getting caught). Deciding whether to respect the copyrights of others is an ethical decision. For more creative people, it's not a hard decision to make; they respect the copyrights of others because they hope that others will respect *their* copyrights. It doesn't necessarily work this way, of course—there's no guarantee that your copyrights are safe because you decline to steal from other creators—but we must remember than any group is made up of its members and that the actions and attitudes of any group are made up of the actions and attitudes of the individuals in it. If you believe that copyright benefits society, as our founding fathers planned, then you must, for the sake of consistency, recognize the boundaries copyright imposes.

Lee Wilson, Fair Use, Free Use, and Use by Permission, *2005.*

Copyright law pertains to "original works of authorship fixed in any tangible medium of expression." Works of authorship include: "(1) literary works; (2) musical works, including any accompanying words; (3) dramatic works, including any accompanying music; (4) pantomimes and choreographic works; (5) pictorial, graphic, and sculptural works; (6) motion pictures and audiovisual works; (7) sound recordings; and (8) architectural works"

Copyright does not extend to: works that lack originality, works in the public domain, U.S. government works, ideas, procedures, processes, systems, methods of operation, concepts, principles, discoveries, or names, titles, and short phrases (e.g., mottoes, slogans). Patent, trademark, and contract law are potential sources of protection for ideas, data, discoveries, or creative slogans that are not protected by copyright law.

Words, Ideas, and "Creative Forms of Expression"

Examples of thoughts that are not creative are "the sky is blue" or "the U.S. Constitution was adopted in 1787." These statements can be made without fear of plagiarism or copyright infringement. They are factual, part of common knowledge, and not attributable to the ideas or creative language of any single individual.

However, if this is written without attribution, "The American Revolution unfolded in a leisurely enough manner to allow Hamilton a fairly rich social life amid the grim necessities of war," it is a different matter. It would represent stealing the ideas and creative language of historian Ron Chernow, from his book, *Alexander Hamilton*.

Plagiarism and Copyright Infringement

Plagiarism is a form of dishonesty because it involves passing off the ideas or creative expression of someone else as one's own; it involves the misappropriation of ideas or creative language without attribution. Copyright infringement is the misappropriation of original authors' original language—their creative forms of expression.

Consider three complementary concepts regarding common-knowledge ideas, original ideas, and original "creative forms of expression" used to articulate these ideas. First, if I wrote "Alexander Hamilton was involved in the Revolutionary War," I would not be plagiarizing or infringing copyright because this idea is in the public domain. Second, by contrast, if I paraphrased Chernow by writing, "Hamilton had some leisure time despite his intensive involvement in the war," I would be using Chernow's original ideas (generated from his original research). As such, I would commit "paraphrase plagiarism" if I failed to attribute these ideas to Chernow.

Third, if I were to use both Chernow's ideas and his actual language, I would commit both plagiarism and copyright infringement. To avoid infringing Chernow's copyright, I must place his language in quotations and cite his original copyrighted work (using the year and page number).

In summary, plagiarism is the use of another person's ideas or creative form of expression without attribution; copyright infringement is the use of another person's creative form of expression without attribution and citation. Plagiarism is a form of scientific misconduct; copyright infringement is a violation of federal law.

What Copyright Protects

The U.S. Copyright Act protects the intellectual property rights of original authors in their creative forms of expression—their creative works. Copyright law accomplishes this by giving authors exclusive rights to their creative works. The phrase "exclusive rights" refers to the legal rights of authors of original works to exclude others from engaging in specific activities. Under copyright law, authors may exclude others from reproducing the work, preparing new versions (derivative works), distributing copies to the public, performing the work publicly, displaying the work, giving permission (a license) to others to use the work, or, finally, from transferring the copyright to others. In short, the U.S. Copyright Act gives authors exclusive rights of ownership in their original works.

When Protection Begins

The law is explicit that "a work is 'created' when it is fixed in a copy . . . for the first time." Imagine that I am working on a manuscript. I save Draft #1 as an electronic file (or as a hard copy). Is this draft manuscript copyrighted? Yes. Assuming my work is creative—and not a merely a list of mundane things to do tomorrow (e.g., "get groceries," "pick up dry cleaning"), or recitative, non-creative lecture notes—my work is protected by copyright the first time it is "fixed" in a "tangible medium of expression." In fact, Draft #1 is the first copy of my copyrighted work, and copyright law gives me exclusive ownership rights—"copy...rights"—in my original work of authorship, whether it is published or not.

What Copyright Includes

If, in my manuscript, I quote the eloquent sentence from Chernow's book (cited above), does my copyright encompass his creative work as well? No, because I am permitted under law to copyright only my creative work, not the work of individuals whom I cite. When I purchased Chernow's book, I purchased a copy of his work, but I did not purchase his copyright. Therefore, my copyright only attaches to those creative forms of expression attributable to me. The quotation regarding Hamilton remains the intellectual property of Chernow—or of his publisher, depending on if copyright was transferred at the time of publication.

Legally, I am allowed to use the quotation from Chernow's biography of Hamilton under the fair use doctrine, which is explained later in this article. When using a long excerpt, a table, or a figure from a copyrighted work in a new work intended for publication, or when distributing substantial excerpts, authors should obtain permission from the copyright holder directly or should pay a royalty to the Copyright Clearance Center [nonprofit organization which facilitates permissions such as these].

When a Notice Is Required

Assume I have prepared a final draft of my manuscript, and am ready to send it out for peer review [part of the sequence of academic and scientific publishing is a manuscript appraisal by similar specialists in the author's field]. Do I need to attach the notice "Copyright © Jennifer Horner, 2004" to my manuscript? Technically, no. Current copyright law does not require a copyright notice. Nevertheless, all authors are well advised to attach it. The copyright notice advises all readers as to whom the author is, and the date of creation (i.e., the most recent date of "fixation" in a "tangible medium of expression").

Nor does the copyright need to be registered with the U.S. Copyright Office. The bundle of rights that are exclusive to the author attach to the work whether it is registered or not. However, if I wish to sue a third party for infringing my copyright, I must register my work beforehand with the U.S. Copyright Office. This is a simple matter, and requires a modest fee.

Transferring Copyright

To be legally effective, copyright transfer must be in writing. All owners of the copyright must sign the copyright transfer. On a single-author work, only a single signature is required. On collaborative works, all authors must sign the transfer, because co-authors are "co-owners" of the copyright. Whereas each may independently use, distribute, and create derivative works from the collaborative work, none may transfer copyright to a third party (such as a publisher) without the signatures of all other authors.

Once the copyright is transferred, the recipient owns all the exclusive rights formerly held by the author. For example, the coverleaf of Chernow's book displays this notice: Copyright © Ron Chernow, 2004, meaning he did not transfer copyright to the Penguin Press. In contrast, the coverleaf of Nadeau, Gonzalez Rothi, and Cross's book, *Aphasia and Language*, displays this notice: © 2000 The Guilford Press.

When to Use Attribution

Imagine using the following language without attribution: "Ethical problems, issues, and dilemmas occur for most people on a daily basis. Whenever we ask the question, 'What should I do?' there is a good chance that an ethical issue or concern lurks in the background" (from Shamoo and Resnik's book, *Responsible Conduct of Research*, 2003, p. 3). Or imagine making a copy of Shamoo and Resnik's book, and selling it to students. The potential risk, in either case, is that the copyright owner, Oxford University Press, might sue me for infringement of its copyright.

In contrast, what if I used, as a title of my new work, "The Cognitive Cloud" (borrowing from G. Albyn Davis's work, originally published in 1989 as "The Cognitive Cloud and Language Disorders" in [the journal] *Aphasiology*). Unfortunately for Davis, he could not sue me for copyright infringement, because copyright does not protect titles, names, or short phrases.

"Fair Use"

The "fair use doctrine" is very important to scientists and educators because, according to copyright law, use of copyrighted material "...for purposes such as criticism, comment, news reporting, teaching (including multiple copies for classroom use), scholarship, or research, is not an infringement of copyright."

Although the law is liberal, it does not give us unfettered rights to use others' copyrighted work. To determine whether an individual's use is "fair" (and legal), a court will look at: "(1) the purpose and character of the use, including whether such use is of a commercial nature or is for nonprofit educational purposes; (2) the nature of the copyrighted work; (3) the amount and substantiality of the portion used in relation to the copyrighted work as a whole; and (4) the effect of the use upon the potential market for or value of the copyrighted work."

For an in-depth discussion of the fair use doctrine, see Circular 21, published by the U.S. Copyright Office. When disputes arise regarding plagiarism, copyright infringement, or theft or misappropriation of intellectual property, an academic honor society—or a court of law—will engage in a fact-dependent inquiry to determine who authored a work, its originality, when the work was created, and the "substantiality" of the alleged infringing use. . . .

A Free Society

Copyright law enumerates specific and exclusive ownership rights to authors of creative literary works. At the same time, out of respect for the value of freedom of expression—encompassing citizens' rights to learn, to read, to know, and to build on the creativity of others—copyright law gives scholars the right to use others' works. To be "fair" to the creativity and to the legal ownership rights of original authors (and the economic interests of publishers), it is essential that professionals and scholars always "give credit where credit is due" by citing original works meticulously, by seeking permission from authors and publishers before using substantial portions of original works, and/or by paying royalty fees before distributing articles and chapters for scientific and educational purposes.

In the United States, copyright protections and freedom of speech go hand-in-hand. The founding fathers of the United States recognized that the freedom to express ideas is a hallmark of a free society. They also understood the need to protect ownership rights in original works of authorship, so as to establish incentives for creativity. These complementary notions regarding liberty and economic interests are fundamental to our lives as citizens of the United States, and especially to our work as students, educators, professionals, and scholars. To preserve the moral and legal rights associated with authorship, it is essential that we credit and cite the ideas and creative works of those who inspire our own creative works.

> "From this point of view, there is ample reason to send our current system of copyright to the scrapheap."

Copyright Laws Should Be Abolished

Joost Smiers

In the following viewpoint, Joost Smiers challenges contemporary copyright laws, arguing that the most vigorously defended copyrighted works are movies, books, and music published by a select number of corporations. This, he believes, keeps weaker cultural activities from entering the marketplace and undermines artistic and creative diversity. Abolishing copyright, he proposes, would normalize the marketplace, breaking corporate monopoly of the arts without hurting the vast majority artists, for whom copyright offers marginal financial advantages. Smiers is a Research Fellow in the Art and Economics Research Group at the Utrecht School of Arts, in the Netherlands. He is also author of Arts Under Pressure: Protecting Cultural Diversity in the Age of Globalization.*

Joost Smiers, "Abandoning Copyright: A Blessing for Artists, Art, and Society," *culturelink.org*, November 25, 2005. Copyright © 1996–2005 Culturelink Network. All rights reserved. Reproduced by permission of the author.

As you read, consider the following questions:

1. In Smiers' view, what is the downside of using copyright to secure investments?
2. Why does Smiers claim that the concept of intellectual property is flawed?
3. Why would abolishing current copyright laws increase artistic expression, according to the author?

A couple of years ago, Carlos Guiterrez, the US Secretary of Commerce, announced a series of initiatives to stamp out the rampant piracy of, among other things, music. Damages resulting from counterfeiting and piracy is estimated to amount to 250 billion dollars annually, in the United States alone. In a press release, he stated, "The protection of intellectual property is vital to our economic growth and global competitiveness and it has major consequences in our ongoing effort to promote security and stability around the world."

Now I must admit that it never occurred to me that copyright could contribute to global security and stability. This is quite an intriguing message—and from a US Secretary, at that! Another aspect addressed by Carlos Guiterrez is, however, more obvious. Copyright has increasingly become an instrument for securing huge investments. In the past decade, it has become one of the major driving forces of western economy, and US economy in particular. This development, however, has a major downside: companies owning massive amounts of copyrighted works can, at their whim, ban weaker cultural activities—not only from the marketplace, but also from the general audience's attention. This is happening under our very eyes. It is nigh impossible to ignore the blockbuster movies, bestselling books and top-chart records presented to us by these cultural molochs, who, incidentally, own almost every imaginable right to these works. As a result, most people are completely unaware of all those other, less commercialized activities taking place in music, literature, cinema, theatre and other arts. This is a tremendous loss to society, because our democratic world can only truly thrive on a large diversity of freely expressed and discussed cultural expressions.

Ever smaller numbers of increasingly large and powerful entities own the exclusive rights to ever more works in the fields of literature, cinema, music and graphic arts. For example Bill Gates, widely known as the founder of Microsoft, also owns a rather less known company by the name of Corbis, which collects vast amounts of images from all over the world; together with Getty Images, Corbis is developing into an oligopolist in the field of photographs and reproductions of paintings—in other words: an entity which has a large amount of control over the market, just as the Stationer's guild had in the sixteenth century. The oligopolist has control over which artistic works we may use for which purposes, and under which conditions, in much the same way Queen Anne had control over printed works.

In most cultures around the world, this state of affairs was, and is, highly undesirable, even unthinkable. Artists have always used and built upon other artists' work to create new works of art. It is hard to imagine indeed that the works of Shakespeare, Bach, and countless other cultural heavyweights could have come into existence without this principle of freely building on the work of predecessors. Yet what do we see happening now? Take, for example, documentary makers, who nowadays face almost insurmountable obstacles, as their work almost inevitably contains fragments of copyrighted pictorial or musical content, the use of which requires both consent from the copyright owner and a fee to be paid. The latter is almost always beyond the documentary maker's means, and the former gives Bill Gates, or any other copyright owner, full rights to allow the use of "his" artistic content only in a way he deems appropriate.

Now where in this scheme of things are our human rights? Human rights should guarantee freedom of communication, and a free exchange of ideas and cultural expressions is what greatly helped build our modern society. This human cultural development will, however, grind to a halt when a mere handful of persons or companies can call themselves "owners" of the majority of pictures and melodies our society has brought forth. This puts them in a position where they alone can dictate whether we can make use of a substantial part of our collective human cultural achievement, and on which terms and conditions. The consequences are detrimental: we are being made speechless; our cultural memory is taken from us and locked away; the development and spread of our cultural identity is stunted, and our imagination is laid in chains by law.

Contrary to what one might expect, the seemingly endless possibilities of copying and sampling using modern digital technologies have so far only aggravated the situation. Publicly offering even a mere second's worth of copyrighted work will almost certainly attract attention from lawyers on behalf of the "owners" of said material. Sound artists, who used to freely sample work from others to build new musical creations, are now treated as pirates and criminals. Whole copyright enforcement industries have emerged, scouting the digital universe day and night for even the smallest snippet of copyrighted work used by others—and those found out, often stand to lose literally everything they have.

Copyright has yet another intrinsic fault which makes it difficult to maintain in a democratic society. Copyright nowadays revolves almost exclusively around so-called intellectual property. This is a problem, since the traditional notion of property is largely irreconcilable with intangible concepts such as knowledge and creativity; a tune, an idea or an invention will not lose any of its value or usefulness when it is shared among any number of people. In contrast, a single physical object, such as a chair, quickly becomes less useful when more people want access to it; in this latter case, the term "property" has a clear meaning and purpose. Unfortunately, in the past decades the legal definition of property has been extended way beyond any physical constraints. These days, almost anything can be someone's property, such as fragrances and colours; even the makeup of the proteins in our blood and the genes in our body cells are being claimed as the exclusive property of one company or another, which can subsequently bar anyone else from using it. It is therefore high time to reconsider the current concept of property.

With regard to artistic works, it is quite conceivable that no single person should have the right to claim exclusive ownership over, say, a particular tune. We all know that almost every work of art, and every invention, is based upon the work of predecessors. Now this doesn't mean we should have less respect for artists creating new works of art based on the work of others, and we're obliged to contribute to artists' well-being and income in our society. Yet rewarding their every single achievement, or reproduction or even interpretation thereof, with a monopoly lasting many decades, is too much, because it leaves nothing for other artists to build on. In fact, even criticizing the artist's work can become rather hazardous, as it "damages" his "property". Unpleasant as this sounds, things get even worse when we consider that the vast majority of copyrighted works is owned by a relatively small group of large conglomerates. These mega-industries create, invent or produce nothing at all, yet demand that artists sign over all rights to their works to them, just for the privilege of having their works distributed.

From this point of view, there is ample reason to send our current system of copyright to the scrapheap. Artists will of course feel threatened by such a bold move. The common perception is that copyright first and foremost protects the well-being and interests of artists. After all, without copyright, they will lose all means of existence, now won't they? Well, not necessarily. Let's first look at some numbers. Research by economists shows that only 10 percent of artists collect 90 percent of copyright proceeds, and that the remaining 90 percent of artists must share the remaining 10 percent of proceeds. In other words: for the vast majority of artists, copyright has only marginal financial advantages.

Then there's another peculiar fact: most artists have entered into some sort of covenant with the cultural industry—as if these two groups have even remotely similar interests! For example GEMA, the German copyright organization, sends approximately 70 percent of copyright proceeds directly abroad, mostly to the US, where several of the world's biggest cultural conglomerates reside. In this process, the average artist is nowhere to be seen.

What is called for, is a way to ensure that artists can make a fair income from their work, without the risk of being pushed out of the market and the larger audience's attention by the cultural industry's marketing power. This may sound rather idealistic, and perhaps somewhat unrealistic, but society's need for cultural diversity should not be underestimated.

The interesting thing is that it is quite feasible for artists to thrive without copyright. After all, copyright is simply a protective layer of armour around a work of art—and the question is whether the benefits of this protection outweigh its drawbacks. Artists, and their agents and producers are entrepreneurs. What then justifies the fact that their work receives vastly more protection—i.e. long-term monopolistic control over their work—than the work of other entrepreneurs? Why can't they simply offer their work on the free market, and try to attract buyers?

Let's try to predict what would happen if copyright were abolished. One of the first effects would be intriguing: All of a sudden, it would be no longer interesting for large cultural industries to focus so heavily on bestselling books, blockbuster movies and superstars. If, in the absence of copyright and intellectual property, these works can be freely enjoyed and exchanged by anyone, the cultural industry giants lose their exclusive rights to works of art. As a result, they will also lose their dominating market position which keeps so many other artists out of sight.

However, at the same we should cut market dominating cultural conglomerates in many pieces. We can't tolerate that just a few companies control substantially the production, distribution and marketing for films, books, music, theatre and design. Abandoning copyright would remove one major support from under the dominance of our current cultural industries, but this does not necessarily mean that their dominance would end. Established industries would still hold the means to large-scale production, distribution and marketing of cultural goods and services in a firm grip; this is one of the reasons for their current success: keeping total control over artistic works from the source to the end consumer, and this distribution model is what largely determines which films, books, theatre productions and image materials we can enjoy.

This concentration of power is undesirable in every branch of industry, but it is particularly detrimental in the cultural field. The tool for cutting those cultural giants in many pieces is competition policy, but this should be done with a cultural perspective in mind. Any form of market domination should be driven out. I could therefore imagine that the cultural market be subjected to competitive law with a strong cultural bias. This relates among other things to ownership of means of production and distribution of cultural goods. Also, legislation may be called for to force large cultural enterprises to (re)present all of the actual cultural diversity being created by both local and foreign artists.

The result will be that cultural markets would become normalized, which would enable more artists to show their

"Jones©, Phipps©, & Rees© Attorneys© Specializing© in© Copyright© Law©" cartoon by Dave Coverly. Used with permission of Dave Coverly and the Cartoonist Group. All rights reserved.

work, make themselves known, and make a fair income from what they produce. This income initially results from being the first in the market with a specific work. But there's another factor contributing to the artists' success. A more normalized cultural marketplace will offer more artists an opportunity to build a reputation, like a brand name, which can subsequently be exploited to sell more works at a higher price. This gives more artists an opportunity to keep selling their works to a larger audience than the current, industry-controlled distribution model. Completely new cultural markets will emerge with the changes that I propose. At first glance, it might be difficult to imagine such new market constellations, because we live in a world in which copyright and the dominance of huge cultural giants seem self evident. They are not. Nevertheless, it is not easy to envision the existence of completely different market relations. However, throughout history we have seen markets change continuously. Why not in the distant future? Market relations can change, radically.

I count four major results of our interventions. First, the scale of cultural enterprises will become substantially smaller. Second, publics will not be terrorised any longer by marketing, and can make their own choices more freely. Third, many artists will have a much better chance to make a living from their endeavours. Fourth, the public domain of creativity and knowledge will be restored.

The first effect we might expect from the proposed radical restructuring of cultural markets is that, with these new conditions, the rationale is lost for cultural conglomerates to make substantial investments in blockbusters, bestsellers, and stars (actually, it is unlikely that those kind of cultural giants will still exist after the introduction of the market regulations I have proposed). After all, by making creative adaptation respectable again and by undoing the present system of copyright, the economic incentives to produce on the present scale will diminish. If we were to commit ourselves to the abolition of copyright and the employment of a truly consequently implemented cultural competition policy, we would bring about an earthquake in cultural markets, in favour of a diversity of cultural expressions.

Corporations would never again reach such an exorbitant size and domination of the market as they do today. Of course, it will not be forbidden, for instance, for a cultural entrepreneur to invest a multitude of millions of dollars or euros in a film, game, CD, or DVD. However, the investment can no longer be made under an endless wall of protection.

The effect is, thus, that not a single enterprise will be able to decisively manipulate the cultural playing field. At the same time, through the abolition of copyright cultural conglomerates will lose their grip on the agglomeration of cultural products with which they determine the outlook of our cultural lives to an ever-increasing extent. They will have to give up the control over huge chunks of the cultural markets.

This has far-reaching consequences for the way publics relate to cultural productions. This is the second effect we might expect. Thus far, the public's guide for making choices was what the marketing of cultural conglomerates offered them, overwhelmingly so, to ensure they did not miss anything. However, in the situation I propose, these conglomerates will not exist and, thus, the public's attention will not be steered in only one direction.

This is a cultural gain, much bigger than we can ever imagine. Publics will need to develop their curiosity. This will be their main compass once the marketing of cultural giants no longer exists to influence their tastes. Curiosity is a most valuable characteristic of human beings. It makes us into self-thinking and reflecting citizens.

When copyright is abolished and when the present cultural conglomerates are substantially smaller in size—that is, are normal enterprises, a level playing field is put in place in which many artistic expressions can find their way to publics, buyers, readers, users, and audiences. This is the third effect of my proposals. There will once again be room in cultural markets to manoeuvre for a variety of entrepreneurs, who are consequently no longer pushed out of the public's attention by blockbuster films, bestseller books, and music, visual arts or design stars. The plenitude of artists will be able to find audiences for their creations and performances in a normal market.

There is not a single reason to believe that there is no demand for such an enormous variety of artistic expressions. In a normalized market, with equal opportunities for everyone, this demand can be fulfilled. It is possible to make a very comfortable living off artistic creations—regardless of the genre to which they belong—without being granted a title of ownership. This increases the possibility that a varied flock of artists are capable of extracting a decent living from their endeavours.

If copyright were no longer to exist, works would belong to the public domain, from the moment of their creation or performance. However, this does not mean that creators, performers and other cultural entrepreneurs would be unable to make a living from their operations and make them profitable. In order to understand this process, we should take into consideration that market relations would also fundamentally change. I discuss this in the book I have written together with Marieke van Schijndel *Imagine! No Copyright. Better for Artists, Diversity and the Economy.*

The substantial gains that are to be realized, after we have implemented my proposals concerning the abolishment of copyright and the establishment of a level playing field, reside in the fact that the public domain of artistic creativity and knowledge will be restored. This is the fourth effect of the changes I propose for cultural market relations. It will no longer be possible to privately appropriate works that in actuality derive from the public domain. We may highly appreciate a new work, but it should remain accessible for further creations, appropriations, and for critique, and also for changes and amendments. Public debate will then determine whether alterations are respectful, and whether the original work commands this respect. If public debate does not materialize, it is a loss for democracy. Independent and well-informed critique must once again come to play an important part. It is only by testing and dissecting works that we can sense value verses mediocrity. Actually, cultural conglomerates lose the monopolistic exclusivity over broad cultural areas because artistic materials are available to all, and there are no limitations on the creative adaptation of art.

An extra benefit of my approach is that the absolute character of property, which wreaks havoc upon our societies, is loosened, and in our case undone. In general, ownership has been allowed to occupy a far too central position in our neoliberal societies. Nevertheless, society needs to become much more vocal about its interests—for example in the social, ecological, and economical sense—and needs to be able to enforce these interests. In our case of cultural entrepreneurship, it is even undesirable from a human rights perspective to have the possibility to vest an exclusive property right on a creation and development in the area of knowledge. What is more, this is unnecessary under normal market conditions.

This proposed model would make a world without copyright not just perfectly imaginable, but also profitable for very many artists, and be a veritable blessing to cultural democracy.

> *"The DMCA represents a tough balancing act, and it is still a work in progress."*

The Digital Millennium Copyright Act Is Effective

June M. Besek

In the following viewpoint, June M. Besek discusses section 1201 of the 1998 Digital Millennium Copyright Act (DMCA), which was enacted to criminalize the distribution and use of technologies that enable easy piracy of copyrighted digital works, including music, movies, and television shows. She counters claims that the DMCA curtails free speech and virtually eliminates fair use, maintaining that it ultimately benefits consumers as well as competition within the marketplace. June M. Besek is the executive director of the Kernochan Center for Law, Media, and the Arts at Columbia Law School and chair of the Copyright Law Reform Task Force of the America Bar Association.

As you read, consider the following questions:

1. What exemptions of fair use of did the Librarian of Congress identify, according to Besek?

June M. Besek, "The DMCA Should Not Be Significantly Changed," *IP Law & Business*, vol. 3, no. 1, January 10, 2003. Copyright © 2008 ALM Properties, Inc. All rights reserved. Reproduced with permission from the January 2003 edition of *IP Law & Business*. Further duplication without permission is prohibited.

2. How does the author belive the DMCA should apply to the replacement parts market?

3. In Besek's view, what are some of the beneficial services that have developed as a result of the DMCA?

The Digital Millennium Copyright Act has its flaws, but so far it has not been the incursion into rights that its critics claim. The most controversial aspect of the DMCA, section 1201, prohibits circumvention of tools that control access— such as encryption—to copyrighted works. The law also prohibits distribution of tools to circumvent access or copy control devices. Critics contend that the section gives copyright owners unprecedented control over the use of their works, and threatens the constitutional rights of users. Some propose creating broad exceptions to weaken the statute. Supporters of the law, however, argue that because of section 1201 we have more and better access to copyrighted works than ever before, and the statute's essential protections should not be cut back. Section 1201 has provided substantial benefits to consumers by encouraging the development of innovative new content delivery mechanisms. The DMCA represents a tough balancing act, and it is still a work in progress. So far the courts and the copyright office, which has the power, every three years, to recommend exemptions in the law, have done a rather sensible job of interpreting it.

Critics have argued that section 1201 chills free speech. But the courts do not read the First Amendment as broadly as the DMCA's critics do. No one has been found liable under the DMCA for talking about circumvention. Instead, liability has been based on circulating complete, functional computer programs. For example, in 2001 in *Universal City Studios, Inc. v. Corley*, the U.S. Court of Appeals for the Second Circuit stopped the distribution of DeCSS, a software utility that unlocks an encryption program. The program protects DVDs from being played in unlicensed devices that allow copying.

The court rejected the defendants' First Amendment arguments and ruled that section 1201 was directed at the functional, nonspeech component of DeCSS and served an important governmental interest (preventing unauthorized access to copyrighted works) without an undue burden on free speech. In 2002 in *U.S. v. Elcom, Ltd.*, a federal district court in California reached essentially the same conclusion.

Opponents of section 1201 argue that the statute virtually eliminates fair use [a set of circumstances allowing the use of copyrighted material]. It does so, they claim, by restricting the availability of circumvention devices and banning the circumvention of access controls. While there are some legitimate concerns about fair use, many of these claims are exaggerated. Much of the debate is really about how convenient fair use should be. Should users be able to easily copy and paste digital materials, or is it acceptable if methods of copying are more tedious? According to the Corley court, "the DMCA does not impose even an arguable limitation on the opportunity to make a variety of traditional fair uses of DVD movies" including comment, quotation, or even copying by means of a camera or recording device. Conceding that the resulting copy would not be as good or as easily manipulated as a digital copy, the court concluded: "We know of no authority for the proposition that fair use, as protected by the Copyright Act, much less the Constitution, guarantees copying by the optimum method or in the identical format of the original."

The *Elcom* court also rejected the notion that the DMCA eliminates fair use. The court conceded that "quoting may have to occur the old-fashioned way, by hand or by retyping, rather than by 'cutting and pasting' from existing digital media." The defendant provided no authority which guarantees "the most technologically convenient way to engage in fair use," the court ruled.

Many critics, however, object to section 1201 not based on any alleged limitation on traditional fair uses, but because the controls restrict their ability to make multiple copies of movies, sound recordings, and books. Much of the criticism is based on a very expansive notion of users' "rights" derived from a liberal reading of the Supreme Court's decision in *Sony v. Universal City Studios* [1984]. But many of these "rights" have been acknowledged by neither the courts nor the copyright office.

In Sony, the Court held that time-shifting (the practice of recording a television program to watch it at a later time) was a fair use. However, as register of copyrights Marybeth Peters recently explained in a congressional hearing, "The Court did not consider whether other activity related to home taping of broadcasts—such as creating a library of recorded shows, making further copies from the initial recording or distributing recorded shows to friends or others—would qualify as fair use. . . . Thus, the suggestion that the Sony decision established a fair use 'right' for individuals to engage in a wide variety of reproduction and distribution activities is simply incorrect."

Access Controls and Fair Use

The relationship between access controls and fair use is a complicated one. A use that would be fair if access is authorized does not necessarily justify access without authorization. In the analog world, you do not have a right to steal a copy of a book in order to quote it. If access controls stand in the way of exercising fair use privileges, the Librarian of Congress, through a rulemaking procedure, has authority to grant exemptions. Recently, the librarian created four exemptions, including one for circumventing the access controls on e-books for the benefit of the disabled, where no existing e-book editions can be used with a read-aloud function or screen reader software.

Critics also like to argue that section 1201 stifles competition. Indeed, it is intended to stifle some competition—that is,

A Stimulus to Both Technology and Marketing Innovation

I have been hearing that the DMCA will stifle technology innovation since the day it was enacted in 1998. But there is absolutely no evidence to support that assertion. In fact, the record supports the very opposite conclusion—the DMCA has been an incredible stimulus to both technology and marketing innovation. Just look at some of the new viewing opportunities that have become available to consumers in [2006]:

• Warner Brothers partners with Free Record Shop using P2P [peer-to-peer] distribution

• Disney offers feature length film on iTunes

• CBS delivers college basketball "March Madness" online

• ABC offers free downloads at ABC.com

• Google Video beta launched—essentially going with a wholesale reseller model—creating an iTunes-like store.

The DMCA may protect old business models, but it also stimulates new business models, and movie studios are at the forefront in the creation of new business models based on innovative technology.

DRM [digital rights management] does not interfere with end-user activities any more than the electronic tags on the dresses you buy at the mall. DRM prevents you from breaking the deal you make, taking something you haven't paid for. If you pay for one copy of a DVD movie, the DRM prevents you from making 50 copies. What is wrong with that?

Fritz Attaway, "'DRM' Protects Downloads, but Does It Stifle Competition?" Wall Street Journal, June 20, 2006.

competition from unlicensed playback devices that circumvent technological protection measures. The Streambox VCR was such a device. In *RealNetworks v. Streambox* [2000] the court enjoined its distribution. RealNetworks's system allowed content owners to encode their works and stream them to users of its popular RealPlayer. Rightsholders could determine whether or not users were permitted to copy streamed works by flipping a switch in the software. But the Streambox VCR faked out the RealNetworks system. Consumers who purchased the Streambox VCR could access content licensed for the RealPlayer without the hindrance of its copy restrictions. The court found the Streambox VCR fell squarely under section 1201, and concluded, among other things, that RealNetworks's security measures factored into content owners' willingness to make their material available.

On the other hand, section 1201 was never intended to stifle competition in the replacement parts market, and its attempted use for this purpose is a troubling development. Recently, Lexmark, a manufacturer of computer printers and toner cartridges, sued Static Control, a rival manufacturer of replacement toner cartridges. Lexmark printers will function only with authorized Lexmark cartridges, identified through an authentication sequence. Static Control developed a replacement microchip that enables unauthorized toner cartridges to function with Lexmark's printers. Lexmark alleged, among other things, that these microchips violated the DMCA. [In 2003] the Eastern District [court] of Kentucky agreed. Although section 1201(f) contains an exception for access to achieve interoperability between independently created computer programs, the ruling found that Static Control didn't qualify because it copied Lexmark's program outright.

A similar issue arose in *Chamberlain Group v. Skylink Technologies*. Chamberlain claimed that Skylink's universal remote transmitter violated section 1201 by circumventing the access control in the receiver of Chamberlain's garage door opener. Recently, the Northern District of Illinois granted summary judgment to Skylink. It concluded that Chamberlain had tacitly authorized the circumvention by failing to notify consumers that they were limited to Chamberlain-manufactured replacement transmitters in a market in which universal transmitters are commonly sold—including by Chamberlain itself.

Lexmark and *Chamberlain*, considered together, suggest that the DMCA does not spell the end of the replacement parts market. In Chamberlain, the court concluded that the replacement transmitter could be marketed; in *Lexmark*, the court might have reached a similar result had Static Control not violated the copyright law to achieve compatibility and exceeded the scope of the DMCA exception. It appears that this issue can be resolved by the courts, but if it is not, a clarification to the statute may be necessary.

There are other potential problems—such as malfunctioning access control mechanisms—with section 1201 that may have to be confronted if they are not worked out in the courts or the marketplace. The Librarian of Congress has granted relief in specific cases where evidence showed this was a problem, but has also indicated that an across-the-board solution is beyond his mandate.

Exceptions to the law may also be necessary for archival purposes. In the most recent rulemaking, the Librarian of Congress [the Library of Congress is charged with the mission to "preserve a universal collection of knowledge . . . for future generations"] granted an exemption for certain computer programs and videogames in obsolete formats in order to facilitate preservation of these materials. It would not be surprising if, over time, technological access controls create obstacles to other legitimate archiving activities. Should the need arise, a use-based exemption would have to come from Congress.

Not Just Crying Wolf

Critics of the DMCA also say the ban on distributing circumvention tools eliminates the practical ability of most people to make authorized uses of copyrighted works. But so far there is little evidence that people can't exercise copyright privileges because they don't have circumvention tools. Perhaps it is because the technological controls in current use are not very sophisticated, or because circumvention devices are still broadly available, despite a few widely publicized cases. Or perhaps it is because there really are alternatives to circumvention. But if a need to amend the law becomes apparent, it would be wise to tread warily: Circumvention devices cannot be limited by purpose, so allowing them for some purposes effectively makes them available for all purposes.

In evaluating whether section 1201 requires amendment (and if so, how to amend it), it is important to focus not only on the restrictions it places on use of copyrighted works, but also on the reasons for its enactment. We must address in a meaningful way the fundamental concerns that underlie the legislation: how do we protect works in digital form and preserve the incentive to invest in creating them?

Copyright owners are not just crying wolf: The enormous popularity of [file-sharing] programs like Napster (in its prior incarnation) and Kazaa suggests that unauthorized copying has become common, and that many users of file-sharing programs do not care whether the works they copy are protected by copyright or not. And while some piracy has always been a cost of doing business, at some point it is unrealistic—and unfair—to expect paying customers to subsidize widespread free use. Critics suggest that copyright owners need to adopt "new business models," but they have not yet proposed a model that meets consumer expectations while still providing a reasonable return on investment. Section 1201 has played an essential role in encouraging the development of DVDs, e-books, and services such as Movielink, iTunes, and Rhapsody. These new content delivery mechanisms provide consumers with an unprecedented range of choices as to when, where, how, and at what price they can experience copyrighted works. There are positive indications that the market is adjusting to accommodate users' privileges (and desires). For example, a number of universities are negotiating agreements to provide music download services to students. Pennsylvania State University recently reached a deal with the new and legitimate Napster service. And a recently announced form of CD copy protection apparently allows consumers to make copies for personal use.

If and when section 1201 is amended, the legislation should be tailored to address specific, identified problems on the basis of sound evidence of harm that outweighs the risks of weakening the law. A broad, all-purpose exemption would eliminate the law's force and defeat its goals.

"Years of experience with the 'anti-circumvention' provisions of the DMCA demonstrate that the statute reaches too far, chilling a wide variety of legitimate activities in ways Congress did not intend."

The Digital Millennium Copyright Act Is Not Effective

Deirdre Mulligan, Nicky Ozer, Nicolai Nielsen,
The Samuelson Law, and Technology & Public Policy Clinic

In the following viewpoint, the Electronic Frontier Foundation (EFF) alleges that the enactment of the the Digital Millennium Copyright Act of 1998 (DMCA), while intended to prevent piracy of copyrighted digital works, has had the opposite effect. The EFF maintains that numerous companies have invoked the DMCA in ways that chill free speech and scientific research, place the fair use of copyrighted digital works under siege, stifle innovation and competition in the marketplace, and displace effective computer intrusion and anti-hacking laws. Founded in 1990, the EFF is a California-based nonprofit advocacy group that aims to protect fundamental rights in the context of technology.

Deirdre Mulligan, Nicky Ozer, Nicolai Nielsen, The Samuelson Law, and Technology & Public Policy Clinic, "Unintended Consequences: Seven Years Under the DMCA," *Electronic Frontier Foundation*, April 2006. Reproduced by permission.

As you read, consider the following questions:

1. In the EFF's opinion, how did the Edward Felten case inhibit technological research?

2. What is the EFF's stance on the fair use doctrine?

3. How did the Chamberlain Group use the DCMA and does the EFF think it was justified?

Congress enacted the [1998 Digital Millennium Copyright Act, or DMCA]'s anti-circumvention [of various encryption and other protection devices] provisions in response to two pressures. First, Congress was responding to the perceived need to implement obligations imposed on the U.S. by the 1996 World Intellectual Property Organization (WIPO) Copyright Treaty [which specifically addressed information technology concerns]. Section 1201, however, went further than the WIPO treaty required. The details of section 1201, then, were a response not just to U.S. treaty obligations, but also to the concerns of copyright owners that their works would be widely pirated in the networked digital world.

Section 1201 contains two distinct prohibitions: a ban on *acts* of circumvention, and a ban on the *distribution of tools and technologies* used for circumvention.

The "act" prohibition, set out in section 1201(a)(1), prohibits the act of circumventing a technological measure used by copyright owners to control access to their works ("access controls"). So, for example, this provision makes it unlawful to defeat the encryption system used on DVD movies. This ban on acts of circumvention applies even where the purpose for decrypting the movie would otherwise be legitimate. As a result, it is unlawful to make a digital copy ("rip") of a DVD you own for playback on your video iPod.

The "tools" prohibitions, set out in sections 1201(a)(2) and 1201(b), outlaw the manufacture, sale, distribution, or trafficking of tools and technologies that make circumvention possible. These provisions ban both technologies that defeat *access* controls, and also technologies that defeat use restrictions imposed by copyright owners, such as *copy controls*. These provisions prohibit the distribution of "DVD back-up" software, for example.

Section 1201 includes a number of exceptions for certain limited classes of activities, including security testing, reverse engineering of software, encryption research, and law enforcement. These exceptions have been extensively criticized as being too narrow to be of real use to the constituencies who they were intended to assist.

A violation of any of the "act" or "tools" prohibitions is subject to significant civil and, in some circumstances, criminal penalties.

Chilling Free Expression and Scientific Research

Section 1201 has been used by a number of copyright owners to stifle free speech and legitimate scientific research.

The lawsuit against *2600* magazine, threats against Professor Edward Felten's team of researchers, and prosecution of the Russian programmer Dmitry Sklyarov [all discussed below] are among the most widely known examples of the DMCA being used to chill speech and research. Bowing to DMCA liability fears, online service providers and bulletin board operators have begun to censor discussions of copy-protection systems, programmers have removed computer security programs from their websites, and students, scientists and security experts have stopped publishing details of their research.

These developments will ultimately result in weakened security for all computer users (including, ironically, for copyright owners counting on technical measures to protect their works), as security researchers shy away from research that might run afoul of section 1201. . . .

Professor Felten's Research Team Threatened

In September 2000, a multi-industry group known as the Secure Digital Music Initiative (SDMI) issued a public challenge encouraging skilled technologists to try to defeat certain watermarking technologies intended to protect digital music. Princeton computer science professor Edward Felten and a team of researchers at Princeton [University in New Jersey], Rice [University in Houston], and Xerox took up the challenge and succeeded in removing the watermarks.

When the team tried to present their results at an academic conference, however, SDMI representatives threatened the researchers with liability under the DMCA. The threat letter was also delivered to the researchers' employers and the conference organizers. After extensive discussions with counsel, the researchers grudgingly withdrew their paper from the conference. The threat was ultimately withdrawn and a portion of the research was published at a subsequent conference, but only after the researchers filed a lawsuit.

After enduring this experience, at least one of the researchers involved has decided to forgo further research efforts in this field. . . .

Dmitry Sklyarov Arrested

In July 2001, Russian programmer Dmitry Sklyarov was jailed for several weeks and detained for five months in the United States after speaking at the DEFCON conference [annual hacker convention] in Las Vegas.

Prosecutors, prompted by software goliath Adobe Systems Inc., alleged that Sklyarov had worked on a software program known as the Advanced e-Book Processor, which was distributed over the Internet by his Russian employer, ElcomSoft. The software allowed owners of Adobe electronic books ("e-book") to convert them from Adobe's e-Book format into PDF files [the Adobe file format invented specifically for efficient dissemination of documents], thereby removing restrictions embedded into the files by e-book publishers.

Sklyarov was never accused of infringing any copyright, nor of assisting anyone else to infringe copyrights. His alleged crime was working on a software tool with many legitimate uses, simply because other people *might* use the tool to copy an e-book without the publisher's permission.

Federal prosecutors ultimately permitted Sklyarov to return home, but brought criminal charges against ElcomSoft. In December 2002, a jury acquitted Elcomsoft of all charges, completing an 18-month ordeal for the wrongly-accused Russian software company. . . .

2600 Magazine Censored

The *Universal City Studios v. Reimerdes* case illustrates the chilling effect that section 1201 has had on the freedom of the press.

In that case, eight major motion picture companies brought DMCA claims against *2600* Magazine seeking to block it from publishing DeCSS, a software program that defeats the CSS encryption used on DVD movies. *2600* had made the program available on its website in the course of its ongoing coverage of the controversy surrounding the DMCA. The magazine was not involved in the development of software, nor was it accused of having used the software for any copyright infringement.

Notwithstanding the First Amendment's guarantee of a free press, the district court permanently barred *2600* from publishing, or even linking to, the DeCSS software code. In November 2001, the Second Circuit Court of Appeals upheld the lower court decision.

In essence, the movie studios effectively obtained a "stop the presses" order banning the publication of truthful information by a news publication concerning a matter of public concern—an unprecedented curtailment of well-established First Amendment principles. . . .

Fair Use Under Siege

"Fair use" is a crucial element in American copyright law—the principle that the public is entitled, without having to ask permission, to use copyrighted works in ways that do not unduly interfere with the copyright owner's market for a work. Fair uses include personal, noncommercial uses, such as using a VCR to record a television program for later viewing. Fair use also includes activities undertaken for purposes such as criticism, comment, news reporting, teaching, scholarship or research.

Unfortunately, the DMCA throws out the baby of fair use with the bathwater of digital piracy. By employing technical protection measures to control access to and use of copyrighted works, and using the DMCA against anyone who tampers with those measures, copyright owners can unilaterally eliminate fair use, re-writing the copyright bargain developed by Congress and the courts over more than a century.

Although the Copyright Office is empowered to grant limited DMCA exemptions in a triennial rule-making, it has repeatedly refused to grant such exemptions for consumer fair uses.

Copy-Protected CDs

The introduction of "copy-protected" CDs illustrates the collision between fair use and the DMCA. Sony-BMG, for example, had released more than 15 million copy-protected CDs in the U.S. market as of early 2006. Although the momentum toward universal CD copy-protection faltered after the Sony-BMG "rootkit" scandal in late-2005 [in which the Sony copy-protection software crippled computer operating systems], no major label has renounced the use of copy-protection on CDs.

These copy-protection technologies are certain to interfere with the fair use expectations of music fans. For example, copy-protected discs will disappoint the millions who have purchased iPods or other MP3 players, despite the fact that making an MP3 copy of a CD for personal use qualifies as a fair use. Making "mix CDs" or copies of CDs for the office or car are other examples of fair uses that are potentially impaired by copy-protection technologies.

Companies that distribute tools to "repair" these dysfunctional CDs, restoring to consumers their fair use privileges, run the risk of lawsuits under the DMCA's ban on circumvention tools and technologies.

Fair Use Tools Banned: DVD Back-up Software

We are entering an era where books, music and movies will increasingly be "copy-protected" and otherwise restricted by technological means. Whether scholars, researchers, commentators and the public will continue to be able to make legitimate fair uses of these works will depend upon the availability of tools to bypass these digital locks.

The DMCA, however, prohibits the creation or distribution of these tools, even if they are crucial to fair use. So, as copyright owners use technology to press into the 21st century, the public will see fair uses whittled away by digital locks allegedly intended to "prevent piracy." Perhaps more importantly, *future fair uses will not be developed* for restricted media, because courts will never have the opportunity to rule on them. Fair users will be found liable for "picking the lock" and thereby violating the DMCA, whatever the merits of their fair use defense.

Copyright owners argue that these tools, in the hands of copyright infringers, can result in "Internet piracy." But banning the tools that enable fair use will punish the innocent along with infringers. Photocopiers, VCRs, and CD-R burners can also be misused, but no one would suggest that the public give them up simply because they might be used by others to break the law.

Fair use of DVDs has already suffered thanks to DMCA lawsuits brought against DVD copying tools. There are many legitimate reasons to copy DVDs. Once the video is on the PC, for example, lots of fair uses become possible—film scholars can digitally analyze the film, travelers can load the movie into their laptops, and DVD owners can skip the otherwise "unskippable" commercials that preface certain films. Without the tools necessary to copy DVDs, however, these fair uses become impossible. . . .

Advanced e-Book Processor and e-Books

The future of fair use for books was at issue in the criminal prosecution of Dmitry Sklyarov and ElcomSoft. As discussed above, ElcomSoft produced and distributed a tool called the Advanced e-Book Processor, which translates e-books from Adobe's e-book format to PDF. This translation process removed various restrictions (against copying, printing, text-to-speech processing, etc.) that publishers can impose on e-books.

The Advanced e-Book Processor allowed those who have legitimately purchased e-books to make fair uses of their e-books, uses otherwise made impossible by the restrictions of the Adobe e-book format. For instance, the program allowed people to engage in the following fair uses:

- read the e-book on a laptop or computer other than the one on which it was first downloaded;

- continue to access the e-book in the future, if the particular technological device for which it was purchased becomes obsolete;

- print an e-book on paper;

- read an e-book on an alternative operating system such as Linux (Adobe's format works only on Macs and Windows PCs);

- have a computer read an e-book out loud using text-to-speech software, which is particularly important for visually-impaired individuals.

Time-shifting and Streaming Media

As more people receive audio and video content from "streaming" Internet media sources, they will want tools to preserve their settled fair use expectations, including the ability to "time-shift" programming for later listening or viewing. As a result of the DMCA, however, the digital equivalents of VCRs and cassette decks for streaming media may never arrive.

Start-up software company Streambox developed exactly such a product, known simply as the Streambox VCR, designed to time-shift streaming media. When RealNetworks discovered that the Streambox VCR could time-shift streaming RealAudio webcasts, it invoked the DMCA and obtained an injunction against the Streambox VCR product.

The DMCA has also been invoked to threaten the developer of an open source, noncommercial software application known as Streamripper that records MP3 audio streams for later listening.

Embed and Fonts

In January 2002, typeface vendor Agfa Monotype Corporation threatened a college student with DMCA liability for creating "embed," a free, open source, noncommercial software program designed to manipulate [proprietary] TrueType fonts.

According to the student: "I wrote embed in 1997, after discovering that all of my fonts disallowed embedding in documents. Since my fonts are free, this was silly—but I didn't want to take the time to. . .change the flag, and then reset all of the extended font properties with a separate program. What a bore! Instead, I wrote this program to convert all of my fonts at once. The program is very simple; it just requires setting a few bits to zero. Indeed, I noticed that other fonts that were licensed for unlimited distribution also disallowed embedding. . . . So, I put this program on the web in hopes that it would help other font developers as well."

Agfa Monotype nevertheless threatened the student author with DMCA liability for distributing the program. According to Agfa, the fact that embed can be used to allow distribution of protected fonts makes it contraband, under section 1201, notwithstanding the fact that the tool has many legitimate uses in the hands of hobbyist font developers.

A Threat to Innovation and Competition

The DMCA has frequently been used to deter legitimate innovation and competition, rather than to stop piracy.

For example, the DMCA has been used to block aftermarket competition in laser printer toner cartridges, garage door openers, and computer maintenance services. Apple Computer invoked the DMCA to chill Real Networks' efforts to sell music downloads to iPod owners. Videogame hobbyists have been sued for trying to improve or extend the capabilities of their favorite game titles. Sony has threatened hobbyists for creating software that enables Sony's Aibo robot dog to dance, and has sued to block software that allows gamers to play their PlayStation games on PCs.

In each of these cases, it was legitimate competitors and innovators who suffered, not pirates. . . .

Apple Threatens Real over Harmony

In July 2004, RealNetworks announced its "Harmony" technology, which was designed to allow music sold by Real's digital download store to play on Apple iPods. Until Harmony, the only DRM [digital rights management]- restricted music format playable on the iPod was Apple's own "Fairplay" format. Although the iPod plays a variety of DRM-free formats, Real wanted to ensure interoperability without having to give up DRM restrictions, and thus developed Harmony to "re-wrap" its songs using the Fairplay format.

Within days, Apple responded by accusing Real of adopting the "tactics and ethics of a hacker" and threatening legal action under the DMCA. Over the following months, the two competitors engaged in a game of technological cat-and-mouse, with Apple disabling Harmony in updates of its iTunes software and Real promising to revise its technology to re-

Bad for Innovation, Entrepreneurship, and Consumers

In the name of fighting piracy, the DMCA gives copyright holders—and the companies that distribute their material—legal tools that can control who makes products compatible with their technology platforms and able to access their content. Examples can be seen in each of the next-generation platforms for video entertainment, including prerecorded home video, cable and interactive television, and even streaming Internet media. Copyright holders have used the DMCA as a contract enforcement tool, promoted criminal actions against programmers who expose flaws in DRM [digital rights management] software, and worked to suppress academic research that affects copyright protection.

Not only is that bad for innovation and entrepreneurship, it is bad for consumers as well. Ordinarily, new technologies allow us to consume media in new ways. The VCR introduced the idea of taping shows for later viewing. The invention of MP3 players like the iPod allowed consumers to put their entire music libraries in their pockets. Software emulators allowed consumers to play games designed for popular consoles like the PlayStation on their computers. In each of those cases, industry incumbents sought to use the legal process to block the technologies, arguing that they violated copyright law. And in each case, the courts rebuffed the industry's efforts, holding that copyright law is designed to promote, not impede, technological progress.

Timothy B. Lee "Circumventing Competition:
The Perverse Consequences of the Digital Millennium
Copyright Act," The Cato Institute, March 21, 2006. www.cato.org.

enable compatibility. In the end, however, Apple's threats of legal action led Real to give up its efforts.

Tecmo Sues to Block Game Enhancements

Enthusiastic fans of the videogames Ninja Gaiden, Dead or Alive 3, and Dead or Alive Xtreme Beach Volleyball managed to modify their games to create new "skins" to change the appearance of characters who appear in the game (including making some characters appear nude). The modifications were add-on enhancements for the games themselves—only those who already had the games could make use of the skins. These hobbyist tinkerers traded their modding tips and swapped skins on a website called ninjahacker.net.

Tecmo Inc., which distributes the games, was not amused and brought DMCA claims against the website operators and tinkerers who frequented it. The suit was ultimately dismissed after the website was taken down and settlements negotiated with the site's operators. . . .

Lexmark Sues over Toner Cartridges

Lexmark, the second-largest laser printer maker in the U.S., has long tried to eliminate the secondary market in refilled laser toner cartridges. In January 2003, Lexmark employed the DMCA as a new weapon in its arsenal.

Lexmark had added authentication routines between its printers and cartridges explicitly to hinder aftermarket toner vendors. Static Control Components (SCC) reverse-engineered these measures and sold "Smartek" chips that enabled refilled cartridges to work in Lexmark printers. Lexmark then used the DMCA to obtain an injunction banning SCC from selling its chips to cartridge remanufacturers.

SCC ultimately succeeded in getting the injunction overturned on appeal, but only after 19 months of expensive litigation while its product was held off the market. The litigation sent a chilling message to those in the secondary market for Lexmark cartridges.

Chamberlain Sues Universal Garage Door Opener Manufacturer

Garage door opener manufacturer Chamberlain Group invoked the DMCA against competitor Skylink Technologies after several major U.S. retailers dropped Chamberlain's remote openers in favor of the less expensive Skylink universal "clickers." Chamberlain claimed that Skylink had violated the DMCA because its clicker bypassed an "authentication regime" between the Chamberlain remote opener and the mounted garage door receiver unit. On Chamberlain's logic, consumers would be locked into a sole source not only for replacement garage door clickers, but virtually any remote control device.

Skylink ultimately defeated Chamberlain both at the district court and court of appeals, but only after many months of expensive litigation. In the words of the court of appeals, Chamberlain use of the DMCA was nothing less than an "attempt to leverage its sales into aftermarket monopolies." . . .

Sony Threatens Aibo Hobbyist

Sony has also invoked the DMCA against a hobbyist who developed custom "dance moves" for his Aibo robotic "pet" dog. Developing these new routines for the Sony Aibo required reverse engineering the encryption surrounding the software that manipulates the robot. The hobbyist revealed neither the decrypted Sony software nor the code he used to defeat the encryption, but he freely distributed his new custom programs. Sony claimed that the act of circumventing the encryption surrounding the software in the Aibo violated the DMCA and demanded that the hobbyist remove his programs from his website.

Responding to public outcry, Sony ultimately permitted the hobbyist to repost some of his programs (on the understanding that Sony retained the right to commercially exploit the hobbyist's work). The incident illustrated Sony's willingness to invoke the DMCA in situations with no relationship to "piracy." . . .

DMCA Shoulders Aside Computer Intrusion Statutes

The DMCA's anti-circumvention provisions have also threatened to displace "computer intrusion" and "anti-hacking" laws, something that Congress plainly never intended.

State and federal statutes already protect computer network owners from unauthorized intrusions. These include the Computer Fraud and Abuse Act (CFAA), the Wiretap Act, the Electronic Communications Privacy Act (ECPA), and a variety of state computer intrusion statutes. These statutes, however, generally require that a plaintiff prove that the intrusion caused some harm. The DMCA, in contrast, contains no financial damage threshold, tempting some to use it in place of the statutes that were designed to address computer intrusion.

Fortunately, the courts appear to be taking steps to reign in this particular misuse of the DMCA, ruling that the use of authentic usernames and passwords to access computers cannot constitute circumvention, even if done without the authorization of the computer owner. Until more judicial precedents are on the books, however, the improper use of the DMCA as an all-purpose computer intrusion prohibition will continue to muddy the waters for lawyers and professionals. . . .

Hindering Legitimate Activities

Years of experience with the "anti-circumvention" provisions of the DMCA demonstrate that the statute reaches too far, chilling a wide variety of legitimate activities in ways Congress did not intend. As an increasing number of copyright works are wrapped in technological protection measures, it is likely that the DMCA's anti-circumvention provisions will be applied in further unforeseen contexts, hindering the legitimate activities of innovators, researchers, the press, and the public at large.

*"Why can't designers beat the pirates?
Since there is no protection for fashion
design in the U.S., companies have
emerged with piracy as their business
model."*

The Piracy Design Prohibition Act Would Protect the Fashion Industry

Narciso Rodriguez

In the following viewpoint, Narciso Rodriguez argues that fashion designs need copyright protection. The Piracy Design Prohibition Act, introduced in 2006, is a pending bill that would grant copyright protection to fashion designs for three years. He claims fashion designers spend years of training and thousands of dollars to create, show, and market their lines only to have pirates, with virtually no overhead and using sweatshop labor, copy them. Narciso Rodriguez is an American fashion designer and a two-time winner of the Council of Fashion Designers of America's Womenswear Designer of the Year Award.

Narciso Rodriguez, Testimony of Fashion Designer Narciso Rodriguez Before the Subcommittee on Courts, the Internet and Intellectual Property Committee on the Judiciary, U.S. House of Representatives, Hearing On Design Law—Are Special Provisions Needed to Protect Unique Industries, February 14, 2008. www.judiciary.house.gov. Reproduced by permission.

As you read, consider the following questions:

1. What personal examples does Rodriguez provide to support his claim that piracy threatens fashion designers?
2. In Rodriguez's view, why does piracy prevent him from starting a diffusion line?
3. How does the author respond to concerns raised by the Piracy Design Prohibition Act?

I am pleased to be here today on behalf of the Council of Fashion Designers of America [CFDA], of which I currently serve on board of directors. The CFDA is a not-for-profit trade association of America's fashion and accessory designers. The CFDA works to advance the status of fashion design as a branch of American art and culture and to help elevate this important American industry.

First I would like to thank Congressmen [Bill] Delahunt [of Massachusetts] and [Bob] Goodlatte [of Virginia] for introducing HR [House of Representatives bill] 2033, the Design Piracy Prohibition Act which protects for a period of three years fashion designs that are deemed unique and original and registered with the copyright office. This is the number one legislative priority of the CFDA and our president [designer] Diane von Furstenberg and we hope it will become law very soon.

It is appropriate that this [2008] hearing falls on Valentine's Day, which marks the conclusion of fashion week in New York. Both events serve to highlight the importance of the more than $350 billion U.S. clothing and accessory industry. More and more young Americans are going into fashion, and America now leads the world in fashion design.

Fashion designers and their stores are all over America. In addition to the jobs directly related to the manufacturing of apparel and fabric, the fashion industry creates jobs in many sectors: printing, trucking, distribution, magazine publishing, advertising, publicity, merchandising, and retail.

An Insult to Common Sense and Decency

The theory that copying actually promotes innovation of designer clothing—because the more common a look becomes, the more the fashion-conscious seek out the next thing—is an insult to common sense as well as to the most elementary decency. To claim that piracy accelerates the fashion cycle is like saying that theft should be encouraged because, by necessity of replacement, it would increase the nation's industrial output.

Alain Coblence,
"Design Piracy Prohibition Act: The Proponents' View,"
California Apparel News, *August 24–30, 2007.*

More Acclaim, More Piracy

The more acclaimed America's fashion designs become, the more they're copied. While the U.S. Chamber of Commerce estimates the lost revenues due to counterfeiting and piracy in the fashion and apparel industry (for 2006) to be $12 billion annually, they also indicate that they believe it may be higher due to the fact that design piracy is not outlawed.

As every counterfeit garment starts as a pirated design, we know the $12 billion worth of counterfeit garments is $12 billion of design piracy. Clearly that's only garments seized, a baseline estimate; as design piracy is not illegal, there are no garments seized and therefore no counting is done. But it's a big problem and it's growing.

I am an American designer with a uniquely American story. As the only son of Cuban immigrants, I grew up in Newark, NJ. My father was a longshoreman who dreamed that

I would become a doctor, lawyer or dentist. But from the time I was a teen, I dreamed of being the next Donna Karan, Calvin Klein or Ralph Lauren.

Becoming one took much more than just suddenly having a brilliant idea, sketching it and meeting success.

- *It took training.* Fashion design is an art that must be learned, just like painting, sculpting, or writing. It took nearly $50,000 in loans and three years to get my degree from the Parsons School of Design in New York. My parents couldn't afford my tuition, so I took out school loans to pay the $15,000 a year. Today tuition is $32,000. After graduating, fashion designers usually train as apprentices. I trained under Donna Karan at Anne Klein, as a design assistant at Calvin Klein and as the designer of the Cerruti label in Paris.

- *It took hard work.* After years as an apprentice and designing for someone else, I started my own company in 1998. Ever since then, I'm always traveling to collect ideas, to see new fabrics, develop unusual yarns and fabrics, and to get inspiration from architecture and different cultures and to sell my designs. A signature of my work is the texture and dimension of the fabric of the garment incorporated into the overall design; we create it much like a painter or sculptor creates.

- *It took financial capital.* To design and fabricate my 250 piece collection it takes six to twelve months. The fall and spring runway shows cost on average $800,000 to stage. The fabric another $800,000, the work room that develops the patterns and garments another $1,500,000. The travel budget for design and fabric development is $350,000 and marketing is another $2,500,000 There are so many aspects of a fashion business that make it risky in the best of circumstances, and the pirates are only making it riskier.

The story I'm about to tell you is one of the reasons that I am before this subcommittee today urging that you pass a law to prohibit piracy of fashion designs. Back in 1996 one particular dress put me on the fashion map. My good friend Carolyn Bessette (whom I met while working at Calvin Klein), asked me to design her dress for her marriage to John F. Kennedy, Jr. That dress became the most copied silhouette of the past decade. The pirates sold around 7 million or 8 million copies. I sold 40.

I used a special technique to complete that look and it is part of my signature style that I had been developing since I was quite young. There was a lot of construction and special placement of seams involved even though it looks quite simple. It's a technique that fellow designers have learned from. The first group of copies the pirates released weren't sophisticated, but then, a magazine reprinted the correct sketch of the dress and far superior copies were produced. Those dresses were sold using my name, and using the Kennedy name. Some may say that I benefited from the publicity; publicity with no sales does not pay the bills.

Not Unique

Unfortunately, this piracy story is not unique. I have many more and so do most designers. Years ago I made a signature handbag. It was knocked off by a manufacturer, and walking down the street before I could sell it. Now that I have the financial backing to create the infrastructure that would be required to put a piece like my signature bag into production—everybody already has it. At 21st and Park in New York a guy stands on the corner and sells copies of it every day. I would love to know where that money is going and what it funds.

The same thing happened with my signature shoes—we call them the Sarah Jessica shoe because Sarah Jessica Parker wore them on [television show] Sex and the City. I was finally at a point in my career where I was able to take a signature look I had worked on for years and produce it for my client. I'd been sketching those shoes, and evolving them since I was a teen. Then the design was knocked off by a manufacturer. There is no way, under the current legal system in the U.S, for designers to beat the pirates to market.

Why can't designers beat the pirates? Since there is no protection for fashion design in the U.S., companies have emerged with piracy as their business model. These companies are built for the sole purpose of copying. They have lots of money to warehouse cheap materials in every color of the rainbow. If I show a black dress in crepe with a turquoise bra in satin, then they immediately cut it in similar fabrics and put it into their stores. Pirates don't have to sell it—they just put it in their stores. It's like the guy who takes the shortcut at the race—we all start at the beginning but he cheats and is the first to walk across the finish line.

With no human or capital investments to make, when pirates copy they spend nothing; they can afford to make the copy in such quantities and low price levels that on just one of my 250 styles they could recoup what I might make on my entire collection. I can't even do a diffusion line, which is a mass market line. It is when a designer takes their own designs and produces them at higher volumes using machine sewing and less expensive fabrics. Designer Isaac Mizrahi has licensed a [diffusion] line at Target. So has Proenza Schouler, among others—but that only happens when retailers want the designer name as well as the design, which they can steal without paying. People have already taken my DNA and diffused it. The pirates are the only ones who can make lower priced versions of my designs.

Not Protected at All

If the pirate enterprises were forced to hire real designers to work there would be more designers, more jobs, and it would elevate real and original design choices for all consumers. Instead, they are creating jobs in sweatshops in Asia where the copies are manufactured.

Sadly, the U.S. doesn't treat designers as well as we are treated in other developed countries with strong fashion industries, such as Europe, Japan or India—all provide 15–25 years of protection for registered fashion designs. Unlike photographers, sculptors, jewelry designers, and yes, even boat hull designers, fashion designers are not protected at all. . . .

Fashion designers aren't working with stones or fiberglass, rather our craft is done with beautiful silks, leathers and wools and yes, even metal. Our work can be as whimsical and imaginative as any other—and copied just as fast as any that already has the protection we seek. I heard there is technology today in China that allows a dress to be made from a photo in record time. Perhaps this explains why the pirated merchandise hits the stores not weeks, but months before mine reaches my outlets.

A century ago the U.S. made a determination that clothing was functional and shouldn't be granted protection. Much has changed in the industry since then. . . . Fashion design has become an art form. We don't think that Congress should protect all apparel. Some of it isn't original or unique. But when a designer creates that look that is special, so special that everybody wants to copy it, he or she should have a small window of protection—we're asking for three years—in which they can develop their idea and get it into the marketplace themselves.

To address some of the concerns we've heard raised about the bill:

- We don't want to prevent anyone from picking up a look. A designer's ability to create a trend is often his mark of success. HR 2033 wouldn't cover any design that had ever been publicly available prior to enactment. There will be a gigantic public domain of designs that we can all use for inspiration. However, I shouldn't have to experience walking down a [New York] street and seeing my original in the store window of a department store and a cheap imitation in the window of another, a dozen blocks down.

- Design piracy protection does not drain the market of accessibly-priced garments; it just assures that the creator of the original design which will serve as the basis for an accessibly-priced garment is the one with the opportunity to manufacture or license that line, not the pirates.

- There is no cause of action created against consumers who buy pirated designs in this bill. The only people who can be sued in a civil action are those who make, made or import, for sale or use in trade, or sell or distribute for sale or use in trade pirated designs. Even then the person must have knowledge, or reasonable grounds to know, that the design was protected and was copied.

- We have identified solutions to the problems of fraudulent registrations and frivolous lawsuits, two of the most frequent objections to the bill as introduced.

- We have clarified the scope of what is protected and developed a more narrow and clear definition of originality.

The American International Property Law Association (AIPLA) has called on Congress to address the problem of fashion piracy. In October [2007] the AIPLA Board passed a Resolution in support of the HR 2033 and [Senate bill] S1957, the House and Senate Design Piracy Prohibition Acts with some minor changes to which we have agreed.

Manufacturers have also expressed some concerns about the bill. Apparel and accessory manufacturers told us they were concerned about the scope of the legislation and the risk of encouraging litigation and to a lesser extent, so were designers. The CFDA has had extensive discussions with the American Apparel and Footwear Association in an attempt to reach a consensus to address concerns we shared. We are hopeful that within the next month, we will be able to jointly present to you the negotiated language. . . . While these changes are important, the underlying structure of the bill has not changed.

Today's hearing is about overall design protection. Other industries may deserve protection, I'm only an expert on fashion. I do know that the fashion industry has been working on fashion design protection legislation for over 3 years. We have worked with others in the industry to develop unified support for a bill. We've done the hard work. We are hopeful that once we have this agreement we won't have to wait for other sectors of business to fall behind protection. We're ready—they aren't. We would ask that the subcommittee [approve] the Design Piracy Prohibition Act [in 2008].

> *"Unlike in the music, film, or publishing industries, copying of fashion designs has never emerged as a threat to the survival of the fashion industry."*

The Piracy Design Prohibition Act Would Threaten the Fashion Industry

Kal Raustiala and Christopher Sprigman

In the following viewpoint, Kal Raustiala and Christopher Sprigman maintain that the Piracy Design Prohibition Act—a pending bill which would give fashion designs copyright protection for a three-year period—would kill the fashion industry. In their view, fashion designers rely on referencing both the designs of their peers and of the past, to which they apply their own creative spin. Most importantly, the authors contend that seasonal trends and the cycle of fashion are dependent on designers taking inspiration from, mimicking, and interpreting others' designs. Kal Raustiala is a law professor and director of the Ronald W. Burkle Center for International Relations at the University of California, Los Angeles. Christopher Sprigman is an associate law professor at the University of Virginia.

Kal Raustiala and Christopher Sprigman, "How Copyright Law Could Kill the Fashion Industry," *New Republic*, August 14, 2007. Copyright © 2007 The New Republic, Inc. Reproduced by permission of *The New Republic*.

As you read, consider the following questions:

1. According to Raustiala and Sprigman, what does copyright law currently protect in fashion?

2. In Raustiala's and Sprigman's opinion, how would the Design Piracy Prohibition Act hurt the fashion industry?

3. How do the authors respond to the assertion that copying hurts some fashion designers?

Not too long ago the world's fashion capital was Paris, and a small group of Parisian designers set trends for well-dressed people around the globe. Today, however, the locus is New York, and the American fashion industry is widely recognized as a world leader. So it's not surprising that New York Senator Chuck Schumer would take an interest in haute couture [high fashion].

Just before the congressional recess [in August 2007], Schumer introduced a bill that he claims would help the U.S. fashion industry by extending copyright law to cover fashion designs. Copyright law currently protects certain embellishments, and trademark law protects labels as well as logos, such as distinctive pocket stitching on jeans. But design—the cut, shape, or overall appearance of a dress or shirt—is not currently protected. A similar bill, titled the Design Piracy Prohibition Act, is under consideration in the House [of Representatives]. Like Schumer's legislation, it would outlaw designs that are "substantially similar" to registered designs.

It may strike many as strange that fashion design is not already covered by copyright law. Many creative industries argue, quite persuasively, that their success requires a certain level of intellectual property protection. Without it, innovation would grind to a halt; creators will not engage in creation if they fear others will steal their work.

But fashion designs never have been protected by intellectual property law and, as it turns out, for good reason. Unlike in the music, film, or publishing industries, copying of fashion designs has never emerged as a threat to the survival of the fashion industry. Indeed, growth and creativity in the fashion industry depend on copying.

Why is that? The answer lies in something that we all know instinctively about fashion. As Shakespeare put it in Much Ado About Nothing, "The fashion wears out more apparel than the man." That is, people don't buy new clothes because they need them—they buy them to keep up with the latest style.

The fashion industry responds to our desires by churning out new designs at a rapid clip. But fashion designers don't maroon themselves on a desert island to create their work. Designers pay close attention to the work of their peers, and they love to mine the past for ideas. When they see something that they like, they copy it—or, in the argot of the industry, they "reference" it. That doesn't mean that they copy point-for-point, although sometimes they do. Much more often, designers take an element of an attractive design, work with it, and turn out something that is in the same style but not identical. Flip through any major fashion glossy and you will see what we mean. In the fashion industry's copyright-free zone, designers and fashion firms are free to take a design they like, put their own creative spin on it, and jump on board what they hope will be a money-maker.

The Fashion Industry's Most Sacred Concept

The result is the fashion industry's most sacred concept: the trend. Copying makes trends, and trends are what sell fashion. Every season we see fashion firms "taking inspiration" from others' designs. And every season we see trends catch on and have a moment of wide appeal, only soon to become overexposed and then die. This fashion cycle is familiar; what is less commonly recognized is that it is accelerated by longstanding

Weak Laws, Strong Innovation

The fashion industry is not alone in its surprising mixture of weak intellectual-property laws and strong innovation: haute cuisine, furniture design, and magic tricks are all fields where innovators produce new work without being able to copyright it. This doesn't mean that we can always do without copyrights and patents, and fashion has unique characteristics that limit the damage that copying can do.... But we should be skeptical of claims that tougher laws are necessarily better laws. Sometimes imitation isn't just the sincerest form of flattery. It's also the most productive.

James Surowiecki, "The Piracy Paradox,"
New Yorker, *September 24, 2007.*

legal rules that allow designers to mimic, play with, and improve upon their competitors' designs.

By allowing the copying of attractive designs, current law fits well with the industry's basic mission—to set new fashion trends and then convince us to chase them. And the trend-driven copying of attractive designs ensures that those designs diffuse rapidly in the marketplace. This, in turn, makes the early adopters want a new style, because nothing is less attractive than seeing your carefully chosen clothes on the backs of the hoi polloi [masses]. In short, copying is the engine that drives the fashion cycle.

Schumer's bill would kill that engine. What works to protect the creative process in film and music will have the opposite effect on the runway. Introduce copyright law into the fashion industry's creative process, and you could ruin a good thing.

To understand exactly how the Schumer bill would effect fashion innovation, it helps to review one basic point about copyright law: It does not simply prohibit "exact" copies. Rather, copyright law makes unlawful any use of a copyrighted work that results in a new work that is "substantially similar" to the old. And the standard for substantial similarity is quite low—over many years, in a large number of cases, federal courts have found copyright infringement in the case of books, photographs, music, and other media where no one would mistake the second work for the first.

If Schumer's bill passes, we will see cease-and-desist letters flying about, and even a flurry of expensive, time-consuming lawsuits with designers arguing over who was the originator of every new trend—and more frighteningly, judges and juries deciding who is right. That's not good for creativity; it's just a distraction. And it's an especially silly distraction in the fashion industry, where every new fashion draws inspiration from fashions that came before. The entire industry engages in recycling, recontextualizing, and reinvigorating the past.

A Cure Worse Than the Disease

Recognition of this fact is one of the reasons fashion design remains, after [over two centuries] of intellectual property law, largely unprotected in the United States. Of the many previous fashion design bills introduced in Congress, not a single one has ever been enacted. And the industry itself is divided on the current bill; while the New York-based Council of Fashion Designers of America is supporting it, the Los Angeles-based California Fashion Association is lobbying against it.

There's no doubt that some apparel designers suffer because of excessive copying. But the industry as a whole is doing terrifically well—it is a $350 billion a year industry—as Schumer himself noted while promoting the bill. Upsetting the fashion industry's successful model of creativity makes little sense. It's a cure that is worse than the disease.

Periodical Bibliography

Thomas Brom   "Fast Fashion," *California Lawyer*, May 2007.

Kevin M. Burke   "Design Piracy Prohibition Act—Finding the
                            Middle Ground," *Apparel*, February 27, 2008.

Michael Fitzgerald   "Copyleft Hits a Snag," *Technology Review*,
                            December 21, 2005.

Mitch Glazier and   "Happy Birthday? The DMCA, or U.S. Digital
Fred von Lohmann   Millennium Copyright Act, Outlined
                            Protections for Intellectual Property in the
                            Emerging Digital Economy," *Billboard*,
                            November 8, 2008.

Timothy B. Lee   "What's So Eminent About Public Domain?"
                            Reason, October 31, 2005.

Pamela A. MacLean   "Digital Copyright Act Needs Rebooting," *Legal
                            Intelligencer*, March 23, 2006.

Heather Meeker   "Only in America? Copyright Law Key to
                            Global Free Software Model," *Linux Insider*,
                            May 16, 2006.

Michael Ryan Patrick   "Unfair Use? Why Internet Search Engines May
                            Have a Right to Your Copyrights," *Licensing
                            Journal*, June–July 2006.

Lisa Person et al.   "From Fashion Catwalks to the Courts:
                            Copyright Protection for Fabric Designs,"
                            Copyright World, April 2008.

George H. Pike   "A Stronger Fair Use Doctrine?" *Information
                            Today*, July–August 2007.

Sascha Segan   "Copyrights—And Wrongs," *PC Magazine*,
                            August 2008.

Joost Smiers and   "Imagine a World Without Copyright,"
Marieke van Schijndel   *International Herald Tribune*, October 8, 2005.

Emili Vesilind   "The New Pirates," *Los Angeles Times*,
                            November 11, 2007.

For Further Discussion

Chapter 1

1. The Copyright Clearance Center maintains that copyright, and its complicated fair use exeption, is frequently misunderstood. Do you think you could make a determination of fair use after reading the definition provided by the Copyright Clearance Center?

2. The Motion Picture Association of America, Matthew J. Oppenheim, and the Software & Information Industry Association claim piracy hurts the film, music, and software industries, respectively. How are the authors' arguments similar or different? Use examples from the viewpoints to explain your answer.

3. Laura Palotie and Alexandra Zendrian assert that antismoking campaigns, along with counterfeiting, have hurt Zippo lighter sales. Do the authors unfairly blame counterfeiting for decreased sales in the United States? Explain your answer.

Chapter 2

1. Do you agree with *Knowledge@Wharton* that peer-to-peer (P2P) networks will become legitimate services for acquiring music, movies, and other digital content? Why or why not?

2. Scott D. Marrs and John W. Lynd argue that most YouTube users upload and use copyrighted videos and other materials in ways that infringe. In contrast, Patricia Aufderheide and Peter Jaszi insist that many of these clips are protected under fair use. Who makes the most compelling argument? Use examples from the viewpoints to support your response.

Chapter 3

1. Do you agree with Ken Hunt that P2P networks will transform the content industries for the better? Why or why not?

2. *Network World* suggests that piracy of expensive software has allowed some companies to achieve innovation. In your opinion, does this justify the use of pirated software? Why or why not?

3. Felix Salmon argues that unreliable data can undermine the credibility of the anti-piracy and counterfeiting advocates. Are the figures that Salmon cites to support his argument credible? Use examples from the viewpoint to explain your answer.

Chapter 4

1. Joost Smiers contends that corporations use copyright laws to monopolize the arts. In your opinion, do corporations monopolize movies, music, and literature? Use examples from the viewpoints to support your response.

2. June M. Besek believes the Digital Millennium Copyright Act (DMCA) is an effective tool for preventing piracy, while the Electronic Frontier Foundation believes it chills free speech and scientific research. Both use the Lexmark and Chamberlain cases to support their arguments. Who uses these examples more persuasively? Explain your answer.

3. Narciso Rodriguez emphasizes that the Design Piracy Prohibition Act does not call for action against customers who buy copycat designs. In your opinion, would penalizing or fining knockoff consumers help solve the problem of fashion piracy? Why or why not?

Organizations to Contact

The editors have compiled the following list of organizations concerned with the issues debated in this book. The descriptions are derived from materials provided by the organizations. All have publications or information available for interested readers. The list was compiled on the date of publication of the present volume; the information provided here may change. Be aware that many organizations take several weeks or longer to respond to inquiries, so allow as much time as possible.

Copyright Clearance Center (CCC)
222 Rosewood Dr., Danvers, MA   01923
(978) 750-8400 • fax: (978) 646-8600
e-mail: info@copyright.com
Web site: www.copyright.com

Founded in 1978, CCC is a nonprofit licensing and permissions organization. The center aims to advance education, innovation, and the free flow of information, while encouraging respect for intellectual property and the principles of copyright. The Web site's "Copyright Central" section offers published reports, tools, and guidelines, and is a source of news on copyright.

Creative Commons (CC)
171 Second St., Suite 300, San Francisco, CA   94105
(415) 369-8480 • fax: (415) 278-9419
Web site: http://creativecommons.org

CC is a nonprofit licensing organization that harnesses private rights to support creativity by increasing the amount of work in "the commons"—work available to the public for free and legal sharing, use, repurposing, and remixing. Like the free software and open-source movements, CC's ends are cooperative and community-minded, but its means are voluntary and libertarian. The organization works to offer creators protection of their works while encouraging certain uses of them— "some rights reserved." The organization's FAQ sheet explains its mission in more detail and provides links to documents explaining the freeware and open-source movements.

Electronic Frontier Foundation (EFF)
454 Shotwell St., San Francisco, CA   94110-1914
(415) 436-9333 • fax: (415) 436-9993
e-mail: information@eff.org
Web site: www.eff.org

EFF is an organization of students and other individuals whose mission is to promote a better understanding of telecommunications issues. It fosters awareness of civil liberties issues arising from advancements in computer-based communications media and supports litigation to preserve, protect, and extend First Amendment rights in computing and telecommunications technologies. EFF's publications include the quarterly newsletter *Networks & Policy*, the biweekly electronic newsletter *EFFector Online*, and online bulletins and publications.

Free Software Foundation (FSF)
51 Franklin St., 5th Floor, Boston, MA   02110-1301
e-mail: info@fsf.org
Web site: www.fsf.org

FSF is a donor-supported nonprofit founded in 1985. FSF has a worldwide mission to promote computer user freedom and to defend the rights of all free software users. In 1984, FSF launched the GNU Project to develop free software for a complete Unix-like operating system.

Internet Society (ISOC)
1775 Wiehle Ave., Suite 201, Reston, VA   20190-5108
(703) 439-2120 • fax: (703) 326-9881
e-mail: isoc@isoc.org
Web site: www.isoc.org

An association of technologists, developers, educators, researchers, government representatives, and businesspeople, ISOC supports the development and dissemination of standards for the Internet and works to ensure global cooperation and coordination for the Internet and related Internet-working technologies and applications. It publishes a monthly newsletter and the *IETF Journal*.

Motion Picture Association of America (MPAA)
Office of the Chairman and CEO, Washington, DC   20006
(202) 293-1966 • fax: (202) 296-7410
Web site: www.mpaa.org

Founded in 1922, the MPAA and its international counterpart, the Motion Picture Association (MPA), serve as the voice and advocate of the American motion picture, home video, and television industries. Its Web site makes available industry reports and some guides on piracy and copyright specifically directed at students.

Recording Industry Association of America (RIAA)
1025 F St. NW, 10th Floor, Washington, DC   20004
(202) 775-0101
Web site: www.riaa.org

RIAA is the trade group that represents the U.S. recording industry. Its mission is to foster a business and legal climate that supports and promotes members' creative and financial vitality. RIAA members create, manufacture, and/or distribute approximately 90 percent of all legitimate sound recordings produced and sold in the United States. Its Web site offers tools for understanding copyright issues as they affect the recording industry.

Software & Information Industry Association (SIIA)
1090 Vermont Ave. NW, 6th Floor
Washington, DC   20005-4095
(202) 289-7442 • fax: (202) 289-7097
Web site: www.siia.net

The Software & Information Industry Association is the principal trade association for the software and digital content industry. SIIA provides help with government relations, business development, corporate education, and intellectual property protection. The association develops best-practice standards for the software and digital content industry, and advocates a legal and regulatory environment that best benefits the industry. Its Web site provides press releases on its activities and many short reports on software piracy cases.

United States Copyright Office
101 Independence Ave. SE, Washington, DC   20559-6000
(202) 707-3000
Web site: www.copyright.gov

The U.S. Copyright Office is part of the Library of Congress. Its mission is to "promote creativity by administering and sustaining an effective national copyright system." The office registers copyrights and provides information on copyright legislation and interpretation, and its archives are a record of the United States' cultural and historical heritage. The office's Web site makes available many reports, studies, and circulars about current copyright issues.

World Intellectual Property Organization (WIPO)
PO Box 18, CH-1211, Geneva 20
    Switzerland
+41 22 338 9111 • fax: +41 22 733 5428
Web site: www.wipo.int

WIPO is an agency of the United Nations dedicated to developing a balanced and accessible international intellectual property system. WIPO was established by the WIPO Convention in 1967 with a mandate to promote the protection of intellectual property throughout the world, through cooperation among states and in collaboration with other international organizations. Its Web site offers resources specifically for students, such as a collection of reports on various types of intellectual property and how they are protected.

Bibliography of Books

Chris Anderson   *The Long Tail: Why the Future of Business Is Selling More of Less*. New York: Hyperion, 2008.

William Barrett et al.   *iProperty: Profiting from Ideas in an Age of Global Innovation*. Hoboken, NJ: John Wiley & Sons, 2008.

David M. Berry   *Copy, Rip, Burn: The Politics of Copyleft and Open Source*. London: Pluto Press, 2008.

James Bessen and Michael J. Meurer   *Patent Failure: How Judges, Bureaucrats, and Lawyers Put Innovators at Risk*. Hoboken, NJ: Princeton University Press, 2008.

Michael Boldrin and David K. Levine   *Against Copyright Monopoly*. Cambridge, MA: Cambridge University Press, 2008.

Chris DiBona et al.   *Open Source 2.0: The Continuing Evolution*. Sebastopol, CA: O'Reilly Media, 2005.

Joseph Feller et al., eds.   *Perspectives on Free and Open Software*. Cambridge, MA: MIT Press, 2005.

Michael Heller   *The Gridlock Economy: How Too Much Ownership Wrecks Markets, Stops Innovation, and Costs Lives*. New York: Basic Books, 2008.

David Kusek and
Gerd Leonhard

The Future of Music: Manifesto for the Digital Music Revolution. Boston, MA: Berklee Press, 2005.

Lawrence Lessig

Free Culture: The Nature and Future of Creativity. New York: Penguin Press, 2005.

Lawrence Lessig

Remix: Making Art and Commerce Thrive in the Hybrid Economy. New York: Penguin Press, 2008.

Jessica Litman

Digital Copyright. 5th ed. New York: Prometheus Books, 2006.

John Logie

Peers, Pirates, and Persuasion: Rhetoric in the Peer-to-Peer Debates. West Lafayette, IN: Parlor Press, 2006.

Matt Mason

The Pirate's Dilemma: How Youth Culture Reinvented Capitalism. New York: Free Press, 2008.

Arthur R. Miller
and Michael H.
Davis

Intellectual Property—Patents, Trademarks, and Copyright in a Nutshell. St. Paul, MN: Thomson/West, 2007.

David J. Moser

Moser on Music Copyright. Boston, MA: Artistpro, 2006.

Neil Weinstock
Netanel

Copyright's Paradox. New York: Oxford University Press, 2008.

Tim Phillips

Knockoff: The Deadly Trade in Counterfeit Goods. Sterling, VA: Kogan Books, 2005.

Matthew Rimmer *Digital Copyright and the Consumer Revolution: Hands Off My iPod.* Cambridge, MA: Edward Elgar Publishing, 2007.

Aernout Schmidt et al. *Fighting the War on File Sharing* (Information Technology and Law, No. 14). West Nyack, NY: Asser Press, 2007.

Richard Stim *Getting Permission: How to License & Clear Copyrighted Materials Online and Off.* Berkeley, CA: Nolo, 2007.

Nóra Szucs *Copyright Barriers of Electronic Commerce: The Past, Present, and Future of File-Sharing Web Sites.* North Charleston, SC: BookSurge, 2008.

Wallace Wang *Steal This File Sharing Book.* San Francisco, CA: No Starch Press, 2004.

Jonathan Zittrain *The Future of the Internet—And How It Must Be Stopped.* New Haven, CT: Yale University Press, 2008.

Index